THE MOVING PICTURE BOYS ON THE WAR FRONT

OR

The Hunt for the Stolen Army Films

VICTOR APPLETON

The Moving Picture Boys on the War Front

Victor Appleton

PO Box 2211
Fairfield, IA 52556
www.1stworldlibrary.com
First Edition

LCCN: 2006907740

Softcover ISBN: 1-4218-2459-0
Hardcover ISBN: 1-4218-2359-4
eBook ISBN: 1-4218-2559-7

1st World Library Literary Society

Giving Back to the World

"If you want to work on the core problem, it's early school literacy."

- James Barksdale, former CEO of Netscape

"No skill is more crucial to the future of a child, or to a democratic and prosperous society, than literacy."

- Los Angeles Times

Literacy... means far more than learning how to read and write... The aim is to transmit... knowledge and promote social participation."

- UNESCO

"Literacy is not a luxury, it is a right and a responsibility. If our world is to meet the challenges of the twenty-first century we must harness the energy and creativity of all our citizens."

- President Bill Clinton

"Parents should be encouraged to read to their children, and teachers should be equipped with all available techniques for teaching literacy, so the varying needs and capacities of individual kids can be taken into account."

- Hugh Mackay

CONTENTS

CHAPTER I

A CALL TO BATTLE

"Come on now, ready with those smoke bombs! Where's the Confederate army, anyhow? And you Unionists, don't look as though you were going to rob an apple orchard! Suffering snakes, you're going into battle and you're going to lick the boots off the Johnnie Rebs! Look the part! Look the part! Now, then, what about the cannon? Got plenty of powder in 'em so there'll be lots of smoke?"

A stout man, with perspiration running down his face, one drop trickling from his nose, was hurrying up and down the field.

On one side of him was a small army composed of what seemed to be Civil War Union soldiers. A little farther back was a motley array of Confederates. Farther off was an apple orchard, and close beside that stood a ramshackle farmhouse which was soon to be the center of a desperate moving-picture battle in the course of which the house would be the refuge of the Confederates.

"The old man is sort of on his ear this morning, isn't he, Blake?" asked Joe Duncan of his chum and camera partner, Blake Stewart. "I haven't heard him rage like this since the time C. C. dodged the custard pie he was supposed to take broadside on."

"Yes, he's a bit nervous, Joe; but -"

"Nervous isn't the word for it, Blake. He's boiling over! What's it all about, anyhow? Is he mad because I was a bit late getting here with the extra reels of film?"

"No, he didn't say a word about that. It's just that he can't get this battle scene to suit him. We've rehearsed it and rehearsed it again and again, but each time it seems to go worse. The extras don't seem to know how to fight."

"That's queer, considering all the war preparations that have been going on here since we got in the game against Germany," observed Joe Duncan, as he made some adjustments to his camera, one of several which he and Blake would use in filming part of a big serial, a number of scenes of which were to center around the battle in the apple orchard. "With all the volunteering and drafting that's been going on, soldiers quartered all over and as thick as bees around the cities, you'd think these extra fellows would know something about the game, wouldn't you?"

"You'd think so; but they seem to be afraid of the guns, even though they are loaded with blanks. Here comes Mr. Hadley again, and he's got fire in his eyes!"

Mr. Hadley, producer of the Consolidated Film Company, approached Jacob Ringold, a theatrical manager who was in charge of the company taking the parts in "The Dividing Line," which was the name of the Civil War play.

"Look here, Jake!" exclaimed Mr. Hadley, "is this supposed to be a desperate, bloody battle, or a game of tennis?"

"Why, a battle scene, of course, Mr. Hadley!"

"Well, I'm glad to know it! From the way most of your people just rehearsed it, I thought I might be in the wrong box, and looking at a college football game. But no, I wrong the college game! That would be more strenuous than this battle scene, at least as far as I've watched it. Can't you get a little more life into your people?"

"I'll try, Mr. Hadley," answered the manager, as the producer walked over to the two boys who stood near their cameras waiting for the word to be given, when they would begin grinding out the long reels of celluloid film.

"This is positively the worst production I've ever been in!" complained Mr. Hadley to Blake. "Did you ever see such a farce as when the Confederates were hidden in the orchard and the Unionists stormed over the stone wall? You'd think they were a lot of boys going after apples. Bah! It makes me weary!"

"It isn't very realistic," admitted Blake.

"Mr. Ringold's talking to them now like a Dutch uncle," observed Joe, as he idly swung the crank of his camera, the machine not being in gear.

"Well, I hope it does some good," observed the producer. "If it isn't better pretty soon, I'll let all these extra men go and hire others myself. I want that battle scene to look halfway real, at least."

"It'll be a failure, I know it will," observed a melancholy-looking man who strolled up at this juncture. "I saw a black cat as I came from my room this morning, and that's always a sign of bad luck."

"Oh, leave it to you to find something wrong!" exploded Mr. Hadley. "Can't you look on the cheerful side once in a while, C. C.?" he asked, forgetting that he, himself, had been prophetic of failure but a few moments before.

"Humph!" murmured C. C., otherwise Christopher Cutler Piper, a comedian by profession and a gloom-producer by choice, "you might have known those fellows couldn't act after you'd had one look at 'em," and he motioned to the mobs of extra men, part of whom formed the Confederate and the other half the Union armies. "There isn't a man among them who has ever played Macbeth."

"If they had, and they let it affect them as it does you, I'd fire them on the spot!" laughed Mr. Hadley; and at this, his first sign of mirth that day, Blake, Joe and some of the others smiled.

"I don't want actors for this," went on the producer. "I want just plain fighters - men who can imagine they have something to gain or lose, even if they are shooting only blank cartridges. Well, I see Jake has finished telling them where they get off. Now we'll try a rehearsal once more, and then I'm going to film it whether it's right or not. I've got other fish to fry, and I can't waste all my time on 'The Dividing Line.' By the way," he went on to Joe and Blake, "don't you two young gentlemen make any long-time engagements for the next week."

"Why?" asked Blake.

"Well, I may have a proposition to submit to you, if all goes well. I'll talk about it when I get this battle scene off my mind. Now, then, Jake, how about you?"

"I think it will be all right, Mr. Hadley. I have talked to my extra actors, and they promise to put more verve and
spirit into their work."

"Verve and spirit!" cried the producer. "What I want is *action*!"

"Well, that's the same thing," said the manager. "I've told them they must really get into the spirit of the fight. I think if you try them again -"

"I will! Now, then, men - you who are acting as the Confederates - you take your places in and around the farmhouse. You're supposed to have taken refuge there after escaping from a party of Unionists. You fortify the place, post your sentries and are having a merry time of it - comparatively merry, that is, for you're eating after being without food for a long time.

"The farmhouse is the property of a Union sympathizer, and you eat all the more heartily on that account. He has two daughters - they are Birdie Lee and Miss Shay," he added in an aside to the moving picture boys. "Two members of your company - yes, I'm speaking to you Confederates, so pay attention - two members of your company make love to the two daughters, much to their dislike. In the midst of the merry-making and the love scenes the Union soldiers are reported to be coming. You Johnnie Rebs get out and the fight begins.

"And let me tell you if it isn't a better fight this time than any you've put up before, you can pack your duds and get back to New York. You've missed your vocation, take it from me, if you don't do better than you have! Now, then, Union soldiers, what I said to the enemy applies to you. Fight as though you meant it. Now, one more rehearsal and I'm going to start you on the real thing."

Under the direction of the assistants of Mr. Ringold, while Mr. Hadley looked on critically, the Confederates took their positions in and about the old house. They rehearsed the merry-making scenes and Miss Lee and Miss Shay took the parts of the daughters of the Union sympathizer. The two girls, being actresses of some experience, did very well, and the extra people evidently improved, for Mr. Hadley nodded as if satisfied.

"Now, then, Unionists, move up!" he called. "March along the road as if you didn't care whether you met Stonewall Jackson and his men or not. Get a reckless air about you! That's better. Now, then, some action! Lively, boys!"

This part, too, went better; and after a little more rehearsal the producer called to Blake and Joe.

"Go to it, boys! Get the best results you can from this mimic battle. Maybe you'll soon be where it's hotter than this!"

"What does he mean?" asked Joe, as he picked up his camera and took his position where he could film the scenes at the farmhouse.

"I don't know," answered Blake, who was to take pictures of the marching Unionists. "Maybe there are more stunts for us to do in Earthquake Land."

"If there are I'm not going! I'd rather do undersea stuff than be around volcanoes."

"So would I. But we'll talk about that later. Say, that looks better!" and he motioned to the so-styled Confederates, who did seem to be putting more life into their work.

"Yes," agreed Joe. "I guess when it comes to shooting, and all that, there'll be action enough even for Mr. Hadley."

A little later the mimic battle scene was in full swing. Hundreds of blank cartridges were fired, smoke bombs filled the air with their dense vapor, and in the distance bursting shells tore up the earth, far enough removed from the positions of the men to preclude any danger.

The Unionists closed in around the farmhouse. Close-up scenes were made, showing Birdie Lee and Miss Shay fighting off their Confederate admirers.

Then came the turn in the battle where the Southern force had to give way.

"Burn the house, boys!" cried their officer; and this would be flashed on the screen later as a lead.

The dwelling, which had been purchased with the right to burn it, was set afire, and then began a scene that satisfied even the exacting producer. Great clouds of smoke rolled out, most of it coming from specially prepared bombs, and amid them and the red fire, which simulated flames, could be seen the Union leader carrying out his sweetheart, Birdie Lee.

Blake and Joe ground away at their cameras, faithfully recording the scenes for the thrill and delight of those who would afterward see them in comfortable theaters, all unaware of the hard work necessary to produce them.

The Confederates made a last stand at the barn. They were fired upon by the Unionists and finally driven off down the road - such as were left of them - while the victorious Northern fighters put out the fire in the house and the scene ended in the reuniting of long-separated lovers.

"Well, I'm glad that's over!" remarked Mr. Hadley, as he came up to Blake and Joe where they were taking their cameras apart in readiness for carrying them back to the studio. "It didn't go so badly, do you think?"

"I think it'll be a fine picture!" declared Joe.

"The last stand of the Confederates was particularly good," observed Blake.

"Good!" cried the producer. "That's a fine line for a leader - 'The Last Stand.' I must make a note of it before I forget it. And now you boys can go back to New York. Have the films developed the first thing and let me know how they have come out."

"They'll probably be spoiled," put in the gloomy voice of C. C.

Mr. Hadley looked around far something to throw at him, but having nothing but his note book, which was too valuable for that, contented himself with a sharp look at the gloomy comedian.

"When will you want us again, Mr. Hadley?" asked Blake, as he and Joe made ready to go back in the automobile to New York, the "Southern" battle scene having taken place in a location outside of Fort Lee on the New Jersey bank of the Hudson River, where many large moving picture studios are located.

"Oh, that's so! I did want to talk to you about something new I have in mind," said Mr. Hadley. "Blake - and you, too, Joe - are you game for some dangerous work?"

"Do you mean such as we had in Earthquake Land?" asked Blake.

"Or under the sea?" inquired his partner.

"This is a call to battle," replied Mr. Hadley. "And it's real battle, too! None of this smoke-bomb stuff! Boys, are you game for some actual fighting?"

CHAPTER II

THE ACCIDENT

Not at all to the discredit of the moving picture boys is it to be considered when it is recorded that, following this question on the part of Mr. Hadley, they looked sharply at one another.

"A call to battle!" murmured Joe.

"Actual fighting?" added his chum wonderingly.

"Perhaps I'd better explain a bit," went on the film producer. "Most unexpectedly there has come to me an opportunity to get some exceptional pictures. I need resourceful, nervy operators to act as camera men, and it is only paying you two a deserved compliment when I say I at once thought of you."

"Thank you," murmured Blake.

"No thanks necessary," responded Mr. Hadley.

"So now I am ready to put my offer into words. In brief, it is -"

At that moment back of the farmhouse (which was partly in ruins, for the fire had been a real one) a loud explosion sounded. This was followed by shouts and yells.

"Somebody's hurt!" cried Mr. Hadley, and he set off on a run toward the scene, followed by Blake and Joe.

And while they are investigating what had happened, advantage will be taken of the opportunity to tell new readers something of the former books in this series, so they may feel better acquainted with the two young men who are to pose as "heroes," as it is conventionally termed, though, in truth, Joe and Blake would resent that word.

"The Moving Picture Boys" is the title of the first volume of the series, and in that the readers were introduced to Blake Stewart and Joe Duncan while they were working on adjoining farms. A moving picture company came to the fields to make certain scenes and, eventually, the two young men made the acquaintance of the manager, Mr. Hadley.

Blake and Joe were eager to get into the film business, and their wish was gratified. They went to New York, learned the ins and outs of the making of "shifting scenes," as the Scotchman called them, and they had many adventures. The boys became favorites with the picture players, among whom were the gloomy C. C., Miss Shay, Miss Lee, Harris Levinberg and Henry Robertson. Others were added from time to time, sometimes many extra men and women being engaged, in, for instance, scenes like these of "The Dividing Line."

Following their adventures in New York, which were varied and strenuous, the moving picture boys went out

West, taking scenes among the cowboys and Indians.

Later they moved on, with the theatrical company, to the coast, where they filmed a realistic picture of a wreck. In the jungle was where we next met Blake and Joe, and they were in dire peril more than once, photographing wild animals, though the dangers there were surpassed when they went to Earthquake Land, as they called it. The details of their happenings there will be found in the fifth volume of the series.

Perilous days on the Mississippi followed, when Blake and Joe took pictures of the flood, and later they were sent to Panama to make views of the digging of the big canal.

Mr. Hadley was a producer who was always eager for new thrills and effects. And when he thought he had exhausted those to be secured on the earth, he took to the ocean. And in "The Moving Picture Boys Under the Sea," the book that immediately precedes the present volume, will be found set down what happened to Blake and Joe when, in a submarine, they took views beneath the surface.

They had not long been home from their experiences with the perils of the deep when they were engaged to make views for "The Dividing Line," with its battle pictures, more or less real.

"What's the matter? What happened? Is any one hurt?" cried Mr. Hadley, as he ran toward the scene of the explosion, followed by Blake and Joe. They could see, by a large cloud of smoke, that something extra-ordinary had occurred. The figures of several men could be noted running about.

"Is anybody hurt?" demanded the producer again, as he and the two boys reached the place. "I'll send the ambulance, if there is." For when a film battle takes place men are often wounded by accident, and it is necessary to maintain a real hospital on the scene.

"I don't believe any one's hurt," remarked Mr. Robertson, who did juvenile leads.

"Unless it might be C. C.," remarked Mr. Levinberg, who was usually cast as a villain. "And small loss if he was laid up for a week or so. We'd be more cheerful if he were."

"Is C. C. hurt?" asked Joe.

"No; but I guess he's pretty badly scared," answered Mr. Robertson. "After this I guess he'll have more respect for a smoke bomb."

"Was that what exploded?" asked Mr. Hadley.

"Yes," replied the "villain." He pointed to Mr. C. C. Piper walking along in the midst of a group of soldiers. "It happened this way: We were talking about the battle scene, and C. C. kept saying it would be a failure when projected because the smoke bombs were not timed right. He said they should explode closer to the firing line, and some of the men who handled them said they held them as long as they dared before throwing them.

"Old C. C. sneered at this, and said he could hold a smoke bomb until the fuse was burned down out of sight, and then throw it and get better results. So they dared him to try it."

"Well?" asked Mr. Hadley, as the actor paused.

"Well, C. C. did it. He held the smoke bomb, all right, but he didn't throw it soon enough, and, as a result, it exploded almost in his face. Lucky it's only made of heavy paper and not very powerful powder, so he was only knocked down and scorched a little. But I guess he'll have more respect for smoke bombs after this."

"Foolish fellow!" remarked Mr. Hadley. "He never will listen to reason. I hope he isn't badly hurt."

"It's only his feelings, mostly," declared the juvenile actor.

Mr. Piper, otherwise called C. C., came limping along toward the producer and the moving picture boys.

"Mr. Hadley, you may have my resignation, effective at once!" cried the tragedian.

"Oh, don't say that, Mr. Piper. You're not hurt -"

"Well, it isn't any thanks to one of your men that I'm not. I offered to show them how to throw a smoke bomb, and they gave me one with an extra short fuse. It went off almost in my face. If my looks aren't ruined my nerves are, and -"

"No danger of your *nerve* being gone," murmured Blake, nudging his chum.

"I should say not!"

"Anyhow, I resign!" declared C.C. savagely.

But, as he did this on the average of twice a week, it had become so now that no one paid any attention to him. Mr. Hadley, seeing that he was in no danger and hardly even painfully scorched, no longer worried about the gloomy comedian.

"And now to get back to what we were talking about before that interruption came," said Mr. Hadley to the moving picture boys. "Do you think you'd like to tackle the job?"

"What is it?" asked Blake.

"Give us an idea," added his chum.

"Well, it isn't going to be any easy work," went on the producer. "And I might as well tell you, first as last, that it will be positively dangerous on all sides."

"Like anything we've done before?" Blake wanted to know.

"Not exactly. Earthquake Land is as near like it as anything that occurs to me. In short, how would you like to go to Europe?"

"To the war?" cried Joe.

"Yes; but to take films, not prisoners!"

"Great!" cried Blake. "That suits me, all right!"

"The same here!" agreed Joe instantly. "Tell us more about it!"

"I will in a few days," promised the producer. "I have

several details to arrange. Meanwhile, I have a little commission for you along the same line, but it's right around here - or, rather, down in Wrightstown, New Jersey, at one of the army camps.

"I can tell you this much: If you go to Europe, it will be as special agents of Uncle Sam, making films for the use of the army. You will be commissioned, if my plans work out, though you will be non-combatants. The war department wants reliable films, and they asked me to get some for them. I at once thought of you two as the best camera men I could pick out. I also have a contract for getting some films here of army encampment scenes, and you can do these while I'm waiting to perfect my other arrangements, if you like."

"Down at Wrightstown, is it?" cried Joe. "Well, I guess we can take that in. How about it, Blake?"

"Sure we can. That is, if you're through with us on this serial."

"Yes. The most important scenes of that are made now, and some of my other camera men will do for what is left. So if you want to go to the Jersey camp I'll get your papers ready."

"We'll go," decided Blake.

Two days later, during which they wondered at and discussed the possibilities of making films on the battle fronts of Europe, the two youths were in Wrightstown.

One incident occurred while they were at work there that had a considerable bearing on what afterward happened to them. This was after Joe and Blake had finished making a fine set of films, showing the drilling of Uncle Sam's new soldiers, the views to be used to encourage enlistments about the country.

"These are some of the best views we've taken yet in this particular line," observed Joe to Blake, as they sent the boxed reels to New York by one of their helpers to be developed.

"Yes, I think so myself. Of course, they're peaceful, compared to what we may take in France, but -"

He was interrupted by the unexpected return of Charles Anderson, nicknamed "Macaroni," their chief helper, who hurriedly entered the tent assigned to the two boys.

"What's the trouble, Mac?" asked Joe, that being the shortened form of the nickname. "You look worried."

"And so would you, Joe, if you'd had an accident like mine!"

"An accident?" cried Blake, in some alarm.

"Yes! At least, he *said* it was an accident!"

"Who said so?"

"That Frenchman!"

"What accident was it?"

"Why, he ran into me with his auto, and the army films are all spoiled - light-struck!"

"Whew!" whistled Blake, and Joe despairingly banged his fist against his camera.

CHAPTER III

MONSIEUR SECOR

Macaroni sank down on a chair. Blake said, afterward, their young assistant gave a very fair imitation, as far as regarded the look on his face, of C.C. Piper.

"Ruined! Just plumb ruined!" murmured Charles Anderson.

"But what happened? Tell us about it!" begged Joe. "You say some one ran into you?"

"Yes. I was in the small auto taking the films you gave me to the station, and I had just about time to catch the express when I saw this fellow turning out of one of the side streets of the camp."

"What fellow?" asked Blake.

"I don't know his name," answered Macaroni. "But he's a Frenchman sent here, I've heard, to help instruct our men. He's some sort of officer."

"And his machine ran into yours?" asked Blake.

"Smack into me!" answered his helper. "Knocked the box of films out on the road, and one wheel went over it. Cracked the box clean open, and, of course, as the film wasn't developed, it's light-struck now, and you'll have to take all those marching scenes over again!"

"That's bad!" murmured Joe. "Very bad!"

"Did you say it was an *accident*?" asked Blake pointedly.

"That's what *he* said," replied Charlie. "He made all sorts of apologies, admitted it was all his fault, and all that. And it was, too!" burst out Macaroni. "I guess I know how to be careful of undeveloped films! Great hopping hippodromes, if I couldn't drive a car any better than that Frenchman, I'd get out of the army! How he has any license to buy gasolene, I can't imagine! This is how it was," and he went into further details of the occurrence.

"I brought the films back, covering 'em with a black cloth as soon as I could," went on Charles; "but I guess it's too late."

"Let's have a look," suggested Blake. "It may not be so bad as you think."

But it was - every bit, and Joe and Blake found they would have to make the whole series over, requiring the marching of thousands of men and consequent delay in getting the completed films to the various recruiting centers.

"Well, if it has to be done, it has to be," said Joe, with a philosophic sigh. "And making retakes may delay us in getting to Europe."

"That's right!" agreed Blake. "But who is this fellow, anyhow, Charlie? And what made him so careless? An accident like this means a lot to us and to the Government."

"I should say it did!" agreed Macaroni. "And it was the funniest accident I ever saw!"

"How so?" asked Joe.

"Well, a little while before you finished these films this same French officer was talking to me, asking if there were to be any duplicates of them, and questions like that."

"And you told him?"

"Yes. I didn't see any reason for keeping it secret. He isn't a German. If he had been I'd have kept quiet. But he's an accredited representative from the French Government, and is supposed to be quite a fighter. I thought he knew how to run an auto, but he backed and filled, came up on the wrong side of the road, and then plunged into me. Then he said his steering gear went back on him.

"Mighty funny if it did, for it was all right just before and right after the accident. He was all kinds of ways sorry about it, offered to pay for the damage, and all that. I told him that wouldn't take the pictures over again."

"And it won't," agreed Blake. "That's the worst of it! Did you say you had seen this Frenchman before, Mac?"

"Yes; he's been around camp quite a while. You must have seen him too, you and Joe; but I guess you were so busy you didn't notice. He wears a light blue uniform, with a little gold braid on it, and he has one of those leather straps from his shoulder."

"You mean a bandolier," suggested Joe.

"Maybe that's it," admitted Macaroni. "Anyhow, he's a regular swell, and he goes around a lot with the other camp officers. They seem to think he knows a heap about war. But, believe me, he doesn't know much about running an auto - or else he knows too much."

"Well, seeing that he's the guest of this camp, and probably of Uncle Sam, we can't make too much of a row," observed Blake. "I'll go and tell the commandant about the accident, and have him arrange for taking a new series of views. It's too bad, but it can't be helped."

"It could have been helped if anybody with common sense had been running that auto, instead of a frog-eating, parlevooing Frenchman!" cried Macaroni, who was much excited over the affair.

"That's no way to talk about one of our Allies," cautioned Joe.

"Humph!" was all Charles answered, as he looked at the wrecked box of film. "I s'pose he'll claim it was partly my fault."

"Well, we know it wasn't," returned Blake consolingly. "Come on, we'll get ready to do it over again; but, from the way Mr. Hadley wrote in his last letter, he'll be sorry about the delay."

"Is he eager for you to get over on the other side?" asked the helper.

"Yes. And I understand he asked if you wanted to go along as our assistant, Mac."

"He did? First I wasn't going, but now I believe I will. I don't want to stay on the same side of the pond with that Frenchman! He may run into me again."
"Don't be a C. C.," laughed Joe. "Cheer up!"

"I would if I saw anything to laugh at," was the response. "But it sure is tough!"

The moving picture boys felt also that the incident was unfortunate, but they were used to hard luck, and could accept it more easily than could their helper.

The commanding officer at the camp was quite exercised over the matter of the spoiled films.

"Well," he said to Blake when told about it, "I suppose it can't be helped. It may delay matters a bit, and we counted on the films as an aid in the recruiting. There have been a good many stories circulated, by German and other enemies of Uncle Sam, to the effect that the boys in camp are having a most miserable time.

"Of course you know and I know that this isn't so. But we can't reach every one to tell them that. Nor can the newspapers, helpful as they have been, reach every one. That is why we decided on moving pictures. They have a wider appeal than anything else.

"So we army men felt that if we could show pictures of life as it actually is in camp, it would not only help enlistments, but would make the fathers and mothers feel that their sons were going to a place that was good for them."

"So they are; and our pictures will show it, too!" exclaimed Blake. "On account of the accident we'll be a bit delayed, and if that Frenchman runs his auto -"

"Well, perhaps the less said about it the better," cautioned the officer. "He is our guest, you know, and if he was a bit awkward we must overlook it."

"And yet, after all, I wonder, with Mac, if it was a pure accident," mused Blake, as he walked off to join Joe and arrange for the retaking of the films that were spoiled. "I wonder if it was an accident," he repeated.

In the days that followed the destruction of the army films and while the arrangements for taking new pictures were being made, Joe and Blake heard several times from Mr. Hadley. The producer said he was going to send Macaroni abroad with the two boys, if the wiry little helper would consent to go; and to this Charles assented.

He would be very useful to Joe and Blake, they felt, knowing their ways as he did, and being able to work a camera almost as well as they themselves.

"Did the boss tell you just what we were to do?" asked Blake of Joe one day, when they were perfecting the details for taking the new pictures.

"No. But he said he would write us in plenty of time.

All I know is that we're to go to Belgium, or Flanders, or somewhere on the Western front, and make films. What we are to get mostly are pictures of our own boys."

"Most of them are in France."

"Well, then we'll go to France. We're to get scenes of life in the camps there, as well as in the trenches. They're for official army records, some of them, I believe."

"And I hope that crazy Frenchman doesn't follow us over and spoil any more films," added Charles, who was loading a camera.

"Not much danger of that," was Joe's opinion.

"Come, don't nurse a grudge," advised Blake.

It was about a week after this that the two boys were ready to take the first of the camp pictures over again.

"Better make 'em double, so there won't be another accident," advised Charles.

"Oh, don't worry! We'll take care of them this time," said Blake.

The long lines of khaki-clad soldiers marched and countermarched. They "hiked," went into camp, cooked, rushed into the trenches, had bayonet drill, and some went up in aeroplanes. All of this was faithfully recorded by the films.

Blake and Joe were standing together, waiting for the

army officer to plan some new movements, when a voice behind the two lads asked:

"Pardon me! But are these the new official films?"

Joe and Blake turned quickly before replying. They saw regarding them a slim young fellow with a tiny moustache. His face was browned, as if from exposure to sun and air, and he wore a well-fitting and attractive blue uniform with a leather belt about his waist and another over his shoulder.

"Yes, these are the official films," answered Blake.

"And are you the official artists?"

"Camera men - just plain camera men," corrected Joe. "Ah, I am interested!" The man spoke with a slight, and not unpleasing, accent. "Can you tell me something about your work?" he asked. "I am very much interested. I would like to know -"

At that moment Macaroni slid up to Blake with a roll of new film, and hoarsely whispered:

"That's the guy that knocked into me and spilled the beans!"

The Frenchman, for it was he, caught the words and smiled.

"Pardon," he murmured. "Allow me to introduce myself. I am Monsieur Secor, and I believe I did have the misfortune to spoil some films for you. A thousand pardons!" and Monsieur Secor, with a quick glance at the two boys, bowed low.

CHAPTER IV

ALL ABOARD

Blake was about to make a sharp reply to the polite Frenchman, when he happened to remember what the commanding officer had said. That was that this man was, in reality, a guest of the nation. That he had come over instructed to give as much help as he could in getting the new soldiers in readiness to go "over the top."

"And so I guess I'd better not say what I was going to," mused Blake. Then, to Monsieur Secor he replied:

"I'm sorry, but we're not supposed to talk about our work without the permission of the commanding officer. You see -"

"Ah, I comprehend!" exclaimed the Frenchman, with another bow - a bow altogether too elaborate, Joe thought. "That is as it should be! Always obey orders. I asked, casually, as I am much interested in this motion picture work, and I have observed some of it in my country. So it was your films that I had the misfortune to spoil? I greatly regret it. I suppose it made much extra work for you."

"It did, Monsieur Secor," replied Joe rather shortly.

"That is the work we are doing now."

"And if you will excuse us," went on Blake, "we shall have to leave this place and go to the other side of the parade ground. I'm sorry we cannot tell you more of our work, but you will have to get an order from -"

"Non! Non!" and the blue-uniformed officer broke into a torrent of rapid French. "It does not matter in the least," he began to translate. "I asked more out of idle curiosity than anything else. I will watch as much of your work as is permissible for me to see. Later I shall observe the finished films, I hope."

"If you don't bust 'em again!" murmured Macaroni, when out of the officer's hearing. "I wouldn't trust you any too much," he added, as he and the two chums moved away to get views of the soldiers from a different angle.

"What's wrong between you and Monsieur Secor?" asked Joe. "I mean, aside from his having run into you, which he claims was an accident?"

"Well, maybe it was an accident, and maybe it wasn't," said Charles.

"But that isn't all. I know you, Mac. What else do you mean?" demanded Blake, as Joe began to set up the camera in the new location.

"Well, I don't want to make any accusations, especially against a French officer, for I know they're on our side. But I heard that Sim and Schloss are pretty sore because you fellows got this work."

"Sim and Schloss!" repeated Blake. "That Jew firm which tried to cut under us in the contract for making views of animals in Bronx Park?"

"That's the firm," answered Macaroni. "But they're even more German than they're Jews. But that's the firm I mean. One of their camera men was telling me the other day they thought they had this army work all to themselves, and they threw a fit when they heard that Hadley had it and had turned it over to you."

"It goes to show that Duncan and Stewart are making a name for themselves in the moving picture world," said Blake, with a smile.

"It goes to show that you've got to look out for your-elves," declared Charlie Anderson. "Those fellows will do you if they can, and I wouldn't be surprised to hear that this frog-eating chap was in with them, and maybe he spoiled your films on purpose, by running into me."

"Nonsense!" cried Blake, speaking confidently, though at heart a little doubtful. "In the first place. Monsieur Secor wouldn't do anything to aid a German firm. That's positive! Again he would have no object in spoiling our films."

"He would if he's in with Sim and Schloss," suggested Joe, taking sides with their helper. "If he could throw discredit on us, and make it appear that we were careless in doing our work, our rivals could go to the war department and, in effect, say: 'I told you so!' Then they could offer to relieve us of the contract."

"Well, I suppose that's true," admitted Blake. "And we haven't any reason to like Sim and Schloss either. But I don't believe they could plot so far as to get a French officer to help them as against us.

"No, Charlie," he went on, having half convinced himself by his reasoning, "I can't quite agree with you. I think it was an accident on the part of Monsieur Secor. By the way, what's his army title?"

"He's a lieutenant, I believe," answered Joe. "Anyhow, he wears that insignia. He's mighty polite, that's sure."

"Too polite," said Macaroni, with a grim smile. "If he hadn't waited for me to pass him the other day he might not have rammed me. Well, it's all in the day's work, I reckon. Here they come, boys! Shoot!"

Blake and Joe began grinding away at the camera cranks, with their helper to assist them. Charles Anderson was more than a paid employee of the moving picture boys. He was a friend as well, and had been with the "firm" some time. He was devoted and faithful, and a good camera man himself, having helped film many large productions.

In spite of what he had said, Blake Stewart was somewhat impressed by what Charles had told him. And for the next few days, during which he was busily engaged on retaking the films, he kept as close a watch as he could on Lieutenant Secor. However, the attitude and conduct of the Frenchman seemed to be above suspicion. He did not carry out his intention, if he really had it, of seeking permission from the commanding officer to observe more closely the work of Blake and Joe. And for a few days before the last of the new films had been taken the blue-uniformed officer was not seen around the camp.

Blake and Joe were too busy to ask what had become of him. Then, too, other matters engaged their attention. For a letter came from Mr. Hadley, telling them and Charles to hold themselves in readiness to leave for England at any time.

"It's all settled," wrote the producer. "I have signed the contracts to take moving picture films of our boys in the French trenches, and wherever else they go on the Western front. You will get detailed instructions, passes, and so on when you arrive on the other side."

"When do we sail?" asked Joe, after Blake had read him this letter, and when they were preparing to go back to New York, having finished their army camp work.

"The exact date isn't settled," answered his partner. "They keep it quiet until the last minute, you know, because some word might be flashed to Germany, and the submarines be on the watch for us."

"That's so!" exclaimed Joe. "Say, wouldn't it be great if we could get one?"

"One what?" asked Blake, who was reading over again certain parts of Mr. Hadley's letter.

"A submarine. I mean film one as it sent a torpedo to blow us out of the water. Wouldn't it be great if we could get that?"

"It would if the torpedo didn't get us first!" grimly replied Blake. "I guess I wouldn't try that if I were you."

"I'm going to, if I get a chance," Joe declared. "It would make a great film, even a few feet of it. We could sell it to one of the motion weeklies for a big sum."

"It's hardly worth the risk," said Blake, "and we're going to have plenty of risks on the other side, I guess."

"Does Mr. Hadley say how we are to go?" asked Joe.

"From New York to Halifax, of course, and from there over to England. They search the ship for contraband at Halifax, I believe, or put her through some official form.

"From England we'll go to France and then be taken to the front. Just what will happen when we get on the other side nobody knows, I guess. We're to report at General Pershing's headquarters, and somebody there, who has this stunt in hand, will take charge of us. After that it's up to you and Charles and me, Joe."

"Yes, I suppose it is. Well, we'll do our best!"

"Sure thing!" assented Blake.

"We will if some ninny of a frog-skinning Frenchman doesn't try to ram us with an airship!" growled Macaroni. He had never gotten over the accident.

"I believe you are growing childish, Mac!" snapped Blake, in unusual ill-humor.

The last of the army camp films had been made and sent in safety to the studios in New York, where the negatives would be developed, the positives, printed by electricity, cut and pasted to make an artistic piece of work, and then they would be ready for display throughout the United States, gaining recruits for Uncle Sam, it was hoped.

Blake and Joe said good-bye to the friends they had made at the Wrightstown camp, and, with Macaroni, proceeded to Manhattan. There they were met by Mr. Hadley, who gave them their final instructions and helped them to get their outfits ready.

"We'll take the regular cameras," said Blake, as he and Joe talked it over together, "and also the two small ones that we can strap on our backs."

"Better take the midget, too," suggested Joe.

"That's too small," objected the lanky helper. "It really is intended for aeroplane work."

"Well, we may get some of that," went on Joe. "I'm game to go up if they want me to."

"That's right!" chimed in Blake. "I didn't think about that. We may have to make views from up near the clouds. Well, we did it once, and we can do it again. Pack the midget, Charlie."

So the small camera went into the outfit that was being made ready for the steamer. As Blake had said, he and his partner had, on one occasion, gone up in a military airship from Governor's Island, to make some views of the harbor. The experience had been a novel one, but the machine was so big, and they flew so low, that there was no discomfort or danger.

"But if we have to go over the German lines, in one of those little machines that only hold two, well, I'll hold my breath - that's all!" declared Joe.

Finally the last of the flank films and the cameras had been packed, the boys had been given their outfits, letters of introduction, passports, and whatever else it was thought they would need. They had bidden farewell to the members of the theatrical film company; and some of the young actresses did not try to conceal their moist eyes, for Blake and Joe were general favorites.

"Well, do the best you can," said C. C. Piper to them, as he and some others accompanied the boys to the pier "somewhere in New York."

"We will," promised Blake.

"And if we don't meet again in this world," went on the tragic comedian, "I'll hope to meet you in another - if there is one."

"Cheerful chap, you are!" said Blake. "Don't you think we'll come back?"

Christopher Cutler Piper shook his head.

"You'll probably be blown up if a shell doesn't get you," he said. "The mortality on the Western front is simply frightful, and the percentage is increasing every day."

"Say, cut it out!" advised Charlie Anderson. "Taking moving pictures over there isn't any more dangerous than filming a fake battle here when some chump of an actor lets off a smoke bomb with a short fuse!"

At this reference to the rather risky trick C. C. had once tried, there was a general laugh, and amid it came the cry:

"All aboard! All ashore that's going ashore!"

The warning bells rang, passengers gathered up the last of their belongings, friends and relatives said tearful or cheerful good-byes, and the French liner, which was to bear the moving picture boys to Halifax, and then to England, was slowly moved away from her berth by pushing, fussing, steaming tugs.

"Well, we're off!" observed Blake.

"That's so," agreed Joe. "And I'm glad we've started."

"You aren't the only ones who have done that," said Macaroni. "Somebody else has started with you!"

"Who?"

For answer the lanky helper pointed across the deck. There, leaning up against a lifeboat, was Lieutenant Secor, smoking a cigarette and seemingly unconscious of the presence of the moving picture boys.

CHAPTER V

ANXIOUS DAYS

For a moment even Blake, cool as he usually was, seemed to lose his head. He started in the direction of the Frenchman, against whom their suspicions were directed, thinking to speak to him, when Joe sprang from his chair.

"I'll show him!" exclaimed Blake's chum and partner, and this served to make Blake himself aware of the danger of acting too hastily. Quickly Blake put out his hand and held Joe back.

"What's the matter?" came the sharp demand. "I want to go and ask that fellow what he means by following us!"

"I wouldn't," advised Blake, and now he had control of his own feelings.

"Why not?"

"Because," answered Blake slowly, as he smiled at his chum, "he might, with perfect truth and considerable reason, say it was none of your business."

"None of my business? None of our business that he

follows us aboard this ship when we're going over to get official war films? Well, Blake Stewart, I did think you had some spunk, but -"

"Easy now," cautioned Macaroni. "He's looking over here to see what the row's about. There! He's looking right at us."

The Frenchman did, indeed, seem to observe for the first time the presence of the boys so close to him. He looked over, bowed and smiled, but did not leave his place near the rail. He appeared to be occupied in looking at the docks and the shipping of New York harbor, glancing now at the tall buildings of New York, and again over at the Jersey shore and the Statue of Liberty.

"Come on back here - behind the deckhouse," advised Blake to his chum and Macaroni. "We can talk then and he can't see us."

And when they were thus out of sight, and the vessel was gathering way under her own power, Joe burst out with:

"Say, what does all this mean? Why didn't you let me go over and ask him what he meant by following us on board this vessel?"

"I told you," answered Blake, "that he'd probably tell you it was none of your business."

"Why isn't it?"

"Because this is a public vessel - that is, public in as much as all properly accredited persons who desire may go to England on her. Lieutenant Secor must have his passport, or he wouldn't be here. And, as this is a public place, he has as much right here as we have.

"And of course if you had asked him, Joe, especially with the show of indignation you're wearing now, he would have told you, and with perfect right, that he had as much business here as you have. He didn't follow us here; I think he was on board ahead of us. But if he did follow us, he did no more than some of these other passengers did, who came up the gangplank after us. This is a public boat."

Joe looked at his chum a moment, and then a smile replaced the frown on his face.

"Well, I guess you're right," he announced. "I forgot that anybody might come aboard as well as ourselves. But it does look queer - his coming here so soon after he spoiled our films; whether intentionally or not doesn't matter."

"Well, I agree with you there - that it does look funny," said Blake Stewart. "But we mustn't let that fact get the better of our judgment. If there's anything wrong here, we've got to find it out, and we can't do it by going off half cocked."

"Well, there's something wrong, all right," said Charlie Anderson, smiling at his apparently contradictory statement. "And we'll find out what it is, too! But I guess you're right, Blake. We've got to go slow. I'm going below to see if our stuff is safe."

"Oh, I don't imagine anything can have happened to it - so soon," said Blake. "At the same time, we will be careful. Now we must remember that we may be altogether wrong in thinking this Frenchman is working against us in the interests of our rivals, Sim and Schloss. In fact, I don't believe that firm cares much about the contract we have, though they have tried to cut in under us on other matters. So we must meet Lieutenant Secor halfway if he makes any advances. It isn't fair to misjudge him."

"I suppose so," agreed Joe. "Yet we must be on our guard against him. I'm not going to give him any information about what we are going across to do."

"That's right," assented Blake. "Don't talk too much to anybody - especially strangers. We'll be decent to this chap, but he is no longer a guest of our nation, and we don't have to go out of our way to be polite. Just be decent, that's all - and on the watch."

"I'm with you," said Joe, as Macaroni came back to say that all was well in their cabin where they had left most of their personal possessions. The cameras and the reels of unexposed film were in the hold with their heavy baggage, but they had kept with them a small camera and some film for use in emergencies.

"For we might sight a submarine," Joe had said. "And if I get a chance, I'm going to film a torpedo."

By this time the vessel was down in the Narrows, with the frowning forts on either side, and as they passed these harbor defenses Lieutenant Secor crossed the deck and nodded to the boys.

"I did not know we were to be traveling companions," he said, with a smile.

"Nor did we," added Blake. "You are going back to France, then?"

The lieutenant shrugged his shoulders in characteristic fashion.

"Who knows?" he asked. "I am in the service of my beloved country. I go where I am sent. I am under orders, Messieurs, and until I report in Paris I know not what duty I am to perform. But I am charmed to see you again, and rest assured I shall not repeat my lamentable blunder."

"No, I'll take good care you don't run into me," muttered Macaroni.

"And you, my friends of the movies - you camera men, as you call yourselves - you are going to France also?"

"We don't know where we are going, any more than you do," said Blake.

"Ah, then you are in the duty, too? You are under orders?"

"In a way, yes," said Blake. "We are, if you will excuse me for saying so, on a sort of mission -"

"Ah, I understand, monsieur! A thousand pardons. It is a secret mission, is it not? Tut! Tut! I must not ask! You, too, are soldiers in a way. I must not talk about it. Forget that I have asked you. I am as silent as the graveyard. What is that delightful slang you have - remember it no more? Ah, I have blundered! Forget it! Now I have it! I shall forget it!" and, with a gay laugh, he smiled at the boys, and then, nodding, strolled about the deck.

"He's jolly enough, anyhow," remarked Joe.

"Yes, and perhaps we have wronged him," said Blake. "The best way is not to talk too much to him. We might let something slip out without knowing it. Let him jabber as much as he likes. We'll just saw wood."

"I suppose he'd call that some more of our delightful slang, and translate it 'render into small pieces portions of the forest trees for the morning fire,'" laughed Joe. "Well, Blake, I guess you're right. We've got to keep things under our hats!"

"And watch our cameras and films," added Charlie. "No more accidental-purpose collisions for mine!"

In the novelty and excitement of getting fairly under way the moving picture boys forgot, for the time being, the presence of one who might be not only an enemy of theirs but of their country also. It was not the first time Blake and Joe had undertaken a long voyage, but this was under auspices different from any other.

The United States was at war with a powerful and unscrupulous nation. There were daily attacks on merchantmen, as well as on war vessels, by the deadly submarine, and there was no telling, once they reached the danger zone, what their own fate might be.

So even the start of the voyage was different from one that might have been taken under more favorable skies. Soon after they had passed into the lower bay word was passed that the passengers would be assigned to "watches," or squads, for lifeboat drill, in anticipation of reaching the dangerous submarine zone.

And then followed anxious days, not that there was any particular danger as yet from hostile craft, but every one anticipated there would be, and there was a grim earnestness about the lifeboat drills.

"I have been through it all before - when I came over," said Lieutenant Secor to the boys; "but it has not lost its terrible charm. It is a part of this great war!"

And as the ship plowed her way on toward her destination the anxious days became more anxious, and there were strained looks on the faces of all.

CHAPTER VI

A QUEER CONFERENCE

Halifax was safely reached, nothing more exciting having occurred between that port and New York than a severe thunder storm, and, after the usual inspection by the English authorities, the ship bearing the moving picture boys was once more on her way.

The lifeboat drills were rigorously kept up, and now, as the real voyage had begun, with each day bringing nearer the dreaded submarine peril, orders were given in regard to the display of lights after dark. The passengers were ordered to be in readiness, to keep life preservers at hand, and were told that as soon as the actual danger zone was reached it would be advisable for all to keep their clothing on at night as well as during the day.

"But the destroyers will convoy us, won't they?" asked Charlie Anderson.

"Oh, yes! They'll be on hand to greet us when the time comes," answered Blake. "Uncle Sam's as well as King George's. But, for all that, a submarine may slip in between them and send a torpedo to welcome us."

"Then's when I'm going to get busy with the small

camera," declared Joe.

"A heap of good it'll do you to get some pictures of it, if the ship is blown up," remarked his chum.

"Oh, well, I'm going to take a chance. Every ship that's torpedoed doesn't sink, and we may be one of the lucky ones. And if I should happen to get some views of a destroyer sinking a submarine - why, I'd have something that any camera man in the world would be proud of!"

"That's right!" agreed Blake. "But don't take any chances."

Joe promised to heed this advice, and he was really enthusiastic about his chance of getting a view of an oncoming torpedo. That he might get views of a warship or a destroyer sinking one of the Hun undersea boats was what he dreamed about night and day.

It was the day before they were actually to enter the danger zone - the zone marked off in her arrogance by Germany - that something occurred which made even cautious Blake think that perhaps they were justified in their suspicions of the Frenchman.

The usual lifeboat drills had been held, and the passengers were standing about in small groups, talking of what was best to be done in case the torpedo or submarine alarm should be given, when Macaroni, who had been down in the cabin, came up and crossed the deck to where Blake and Joe were talking to two young ladies, to whom they had been introduced by the captain.

By one of the many signs in use among moving picture camera men, which take the place of words when they are busy at the films, Macaroni gave the two chums to understand he wanted to speak to them privately and at once. The two partners remained a little longer in conversation, and then, making their excuses, followed their helper to a secluded spot.

"What's up?" demanded Joe. "Have you made some views of a torpedo?"

"Or seen a periscope?" asked Blake.

"Neither one," Charlie answered. "But if you want to see something that will open your eyes come below."

His manner was so earnest and strange, and he seemed so moved by what he had evidently seen, that Blake and Joe, asking no further questions, followed him.

"What is it?" Joe demanded, as they were about to enter their cabin, one occupied by the three of them.

"Look there!" whispered the helper, as he pointed to a mirror on their wall.

Blake and Joe saw something which made them open their eyes. It was the reflection of a strange conference taking place in the stateroom across the passageway from them, a conference of which a view was possible because of open transoms in both staterooms and mirrors so arranged that what took place in the one across the corridor was visible to the boys, yet they remained hidden themselves.

Blake and Joe saw two men with heads close together

over a small table in the center of the opposite stateroom. The tilted mirror transferred the view into their own looking-glass. The men appeared to be examining a map, or, at any rate, some paper, and their manner was secretive, alone though they were.

But it was not so much the manner of the men as it was the identity of one that aroused the curiosity and fear of the moving picture boys - curiosity as to what might be the subject of the queer conference, and fear as to the result of it.

For one of the men was Lieutenant Secor, the Frenchman, and the other was a passenger who, though claiming to be a wealthy Hebrew with American citizenship, was, so the boys believed, thoroughly German. He was down on the passenger list as Levi Labenstein, and he did bear some resemblance to a Jew, but his talk had the unmistakable German accent.

Not that there are not German Jews, but their tongue has not the knack of the pure, guttural German of Prussia. And this man's voice had none of the nasal, throaty tones of Yiddish.

"Whew!" whistled Joe, as he and Blake looked into the tell-tale mirror. "That looks bad!"

"Hush!" cautioned Blake. "The transoms are open and he may hear you."

But a look into the reflecting glasses showed that the two men - the Frenchman and the German - had not looked up from their eager poring over the map, or whatever paper was between them.

"How long have they been this way?" asked Blake, in a whisper, of Charlie.

"I don't know," Macaroni answered. "I happened to see them when I came down to get something, and after I'd watched them a while I went to tell you."

"I'm glad you did," went on Blake; "though I don't know what it means - if it means anything."

"It means something, all right," declared Joe, and he, like the others, was careful to keep his voice low-pitched. "It means treason, if I'm any judge!"

"Treason?" repeated Blake.

"Yes; wouldn't you call it that if you saw one of our army officers having a secret talk with a German enemy?"

"I suppose so," assented Blake. "And yet Lieutenant Secor isn't one of our officers."

"No, but he's been in our camps, and he's been a guest of Uncle Sam. He's been in a position to spy out some of the army secrets, and now we see him talking to this German."

"But this man may *not* be a subject of the Kaiser," said Blake.

"Sure he is!" declared Charlie. "He's no more a real Jew than I am! He's a Teuton! Germany has no love for the Jews, and they don't have any use for the Huns. Take my word for it, fellows, there's something wrong going on here."

"It may be," admitted Blake; "but does it concern us?"

"Of course it does!" declared Joe. "This Frenchman may be betraying some of Uncle Sam's secrets to the enemy - not only our enemy, but the enemy of his own country."

"Yes, I suppose there are traitorous Frenchmen," said Blake slowly, "but they are mighty few."

"But this means something!" declared Macaroni.

And Blake, slow as he was sometimes in forming an opinion, could not but agree with him.

In silence the boys watched the two men at their queer conference. The tilted mirrors - one in each stateroom - gave a perfect view of what went on between the Frenchman and the German, as the boys preferred to think Labenstein, but the watchers themselves were not observed. This they could make sure of, for several times one or the other of the men across the corridor looked up, and full into the mirror on their own wall, but they gave no indication of observing anything out of the ordinary.

The mirrors were fastened in a tilted position to prevent them from swinging as the ship rolled, and as they did not sway there was an unchanged view to be had.

"I wonder what they're saying," observed Blake.

They could only guess, however, for though the men talked rapidly and eagerly, as evidenced by their gestures, what they said was not audible. Though both transoms were open, no sound came from the room opposite where the boys were gathered. The men spoke too low for that.

"I guess they know it's dangerous to be found out," said Joe.

"But we ought to find out what it's about!" declared Macaroni.

"Yes, I think we ought," assented Blake. "This Frenchman has been in our country, going about from camp to camp according to his own story, and he must have picked up a lot of information."

"And he knows about our pictures, too!"

"Well, I don't imagine what we have taken, so far, will be of any great value to Germany, assuming that Lieutenant Secor is a spy and has told about them," Blake said.

"We've got to find out something about this, though, haven't we?" asked Joe.

"I think we ought to try," agreed his chum. "Perhaps we should tell Captain Merceau. He's a Frenchman, and will know how to deal with Secor."

"Good idea!" exclaimed Joe. "If we could only get him down here to see what we've seen, it would clinch matters. I wonder -"

But Joe ceased talking at a motion from Blake, who silently pointed at the mirror. In that way they saw the reflection of the men in the other cabin. They arose from their seats at the table, and the map or whatever papers they had been looking at, were put away quietly in the Frenchman's pocket.

He and the German, as the boys decided to call Labenstein, spoke in whispers once more, and then shook hands, as if to seal some pact.

Then, as the boys watched, Lieutenant Secor opened the door of the stateroom, which had been locked. He stepped out into the corridor, and was now lost to view.

The next moment, to the surprise of Blake and his two friends, there came a knock on their own door, and a voice asked:

"Are you within, young gentlemen of the cameras? I am Lieutenant Secor!"

CHAPTER VII

"PERISCOPE AHOY!"

Sudden and unexpected was the knocking, and it found the boys unready to answer it. They had no idea that the conspirators - either or both of them - would come directly from their conference to the room where a watch had been kept on them.

"Do you think he saw us?" asked Joe, in a whisper.

"S'posing he did?" demanded Charlie. "We have the goods on him, all right."

Blake held up a hand to enjoin silence, though the remarks of his friends had been made in the lowest of tones.

The knock was given again, and the voice of the Frenchman asked:

"Are you within, my friends of the camera? I wish to speak with you!"

"One moment!" called Blake, in a tone he tried to make pleasant. Then he motioned to Joe and Charlie to seem to be busy over the midget camera, which was kept ready for instant use. At the same moment Blake threw a black focusing cloth over the mirror, for he thought the Frenchman might notice that it was in a position to reflect whatever took place in the opposite room.

"Act natural - as if you were getting ready to make some pictures," Blake whispered in Joe's ear, and then opened the door.

"Pardon me for disturbing you," began Lieutenant Secor, "but I have just come down from on deck. They are having a special lifeboat drill, and I thought perhaps you might like to get some views of it. Also, I have a favor to ask of you."

"Come in," said Blake, as he opened the door wider. At the same time he noticed that the door of the stateroom across the corridor was shut.

"Just came down from deck, did he?" mused Joe, as he took note of the Frenchman's false statement. "Well, he must have run up and run down again in jig fashion to be able to do that. I wonder what he wants to ask us?"

Joe and Charlie pretended to be adjusting the small camera, and Blake smiled a welcome he did not feel. Black suspicion was in his heart against the Frenchman. An open enemy Blake could understand, but not a spy or a traitor.

"I thought perhaps you might like to get some of the views from on deck," went on Lieutenant Secor, smiling his white-toothed smile. "They are even lowering boats into the water - a realistic drill!"

Blake looked at Joe as much as to ask if it would be

advisable to get some views. At the same time Blake made a sign which Joe interpreted to mean:

"Go up on deck and see what's going on - you and Charlie. I'll take care of him down here."

"Come on!" Joe remarked to their helper, as he gathered up the small camera. "We'll take this in."

"I thought you might like it," said the Frenchman. "That's why I hurried down to tell you."

"Now I wonder," thought Blake to himself, as Joe made ready to leave, "why he thinks it worth his while to tell that untruth? What is his game?"

At the same time an uneasy thought came to Joe.

"If we go up and leave Blake alone with this fellow, may not something happen? Perhaps he'll attack Blake!"

But that thought no sooner came than it was dismissed, for, Joe reasoned, what harm could happen to his chum, who was well able to take care of himself? True, the Frenchman might be armed, but so was Blake. Then, too, there could be no object in attacking Blake. He had little of value on his person, and the films and cameras were not in the stateroom. And there were no films of any value as yet, either.

"Guess I'm doing too much imagining," said Joe to himself. "This fellow may be a plotter and a spy in German pay - and I haven't any doubt but what he is - but I reckon Blake can look after himself. Anyhow, he wants me to leave Secor to him, and I'll do it. But not too long!"

So Joe and Charlie, taking the small camera with them, went up on deck. There they did find an unusual lifeboat drill going on. The danger zone was now so close that Captain Merceau and his officers of the ship were taking no chances. They wanted to be prepared for the worst, and so they had the men passengers practise getting into the boats, which were lowered into the water and rowed a short distance away from the ship.

The women and children, of whom there were a few on board, watched from the decks, taking note of how to get into the boats, and how best to act once they were in their places.

"Going to film this?" asked Charlie of Joe.

"No, I think not," was the answer. "It's interesting, but there have been lots of drills like it. If it were the real thing, now, I'd shoot; but I'm going to save the film on the chance of getting a sub or a torpedo. This is a sort of bluff on the part of you and me, anyhow. Blake wanted to get us out of the cabin while he tackled Secor, I reckon. What *his* game is I don't know."

"I can come pretty near to guessing," said Macaroni, as he stretched his lank legs, which had, in part, earned him the nickname. "That fake lieutenant is planning some game with the German spy, that's his game."

"Maybe," admitted Joe. "But I don't see how we figure in it."

"Perhaps we will after we've gotten some reels of

valuable film," suggested Charlie. "Don't crow until you've ground out the last bit of footage."

"No, that's right. Look, that boat's going to spill if I'm any judge!"

Excited shouts and a confusion of orders drew the attention of the boys and many others to a lifeboat where, amidships on the port side, it was being lowered away as part of the drill. There were a number of sailors in it - part of the crew - and, as Joe and Charlie watched, one of the falls became jammed with the result that the stern of the boat was suddenly lowered while the bow was held in place.

As might have been expected, the sudden tilting of the boat at an acute angle threw the occupants all into one end. There were yells and shouts, and then came splashes, as one after another fell into the ocean.

Women and children screamed and men hoarsely called to one another. For a moment it looked as though the safety drill would result in a tragedy, and then shrill laughter from the men who had fallen into the water, as well as cries of merriment from those who still clung to the boat, showed that, if not intended as a joke, the happening had been turned into one.

The sailors were all good swimmers, the day was sunny and the water warm, and in a short time another boat had been rowed to the scene of the upset, and those who went overboard were picked up, still laughing.

"I might have taken that if I had known they were going to pull a stunt like that," said Joe, a bit regretfully. "However, I guess we'll get all the excitement we want when we get to the war front."

"I believe you!" exclaimed Charlie. "There's our German spy," he added, pointing to the dark-complexioned and bearded man who had been seen, through the mirrors' reflections, talking to the Frenchman. He had evidently hurried up on deck to ascertain the cause of the confusion, for he was without collar or tie.

The boat was righted, the wet sailors went laughing below to change into dry garments, and the passengers resumed their usual occupations which, in the main, consisted of nervously watching the heaving waves for a sight of a periscope, or a wake of bubbles that might tell of an on-speeding torpedo.

Mr. Labenstein, to credit him with the name on the passenger list, gave a look around, and, seeing that there was no danger, at once went below again.

"Wonder how Blake's making out?" asked Charlie of Joe, as they walked the deck. "Do you think we'd better go down?"

"Not until we get some word from him. Hello! Here he is now!" and Joe pointed to their friend coming toward them.

"Well?" asked Joe significantly.

"Nothing much," answered Blake. "He was as nice and affable as he always is. Just talked about the war in general terms. Said the Allies and Uncle Sam were sure to win."

"Did he want anything?" asked Charlie. "He said he was going to ask a favor, you know."

"Well, he hinted for information as to what we were going to do on the other side, but I didn't give him any satisfaction. Then he wanted to know whether we would consider an offer from the French Government."

"What'd you say to that?"

"I didn't give him a direct answer. Said I'd think about it. I thought it best to string him along. No telling what may be behind it all."

"You're right," agreed Joe. "Lieutenant Secor will bear watching. Did he have any idea we were observing him?"

"I think not. If he did, he didn't let on. But I thought sure, when he came across the corridor and knocked, that he'd discovered us."

"So did I, and I was all ready to bluff him out. But we'll have to be on the watch, and especially on the other side."

"What do you mean?" asked Blake.

"Well, I have an idea he's after our films, the same as he was before, either to spoil them or get them for some purpose of his own. Just now we aren't taking any, and he hasn't any desire, I suppose, to get possession of the unexposed reels. But when we begin to make pictures of our boys in the trenches, and perhaps of some engagements, we'll have to see that the reels are well guarded."

"We will," agreed Blake. "What was going on up here? We heard a racket, and Labenstein rushed up half dressed."

"Lifeboat spilled - no harm done," explained Charlie. "Well, I might as well take this camera below if we're not going to use it."

"Come on, Blake," urged Joe. "They're going to have gun drill. Let's watch."

The vessel carried four quick-firing guns for use against submarines, one each in the bow and stern, and one on either beam. The gunners were from Uncle Sam's navy and were expert marksmen, as had been evidenced in practice.

"Are we in the danger zone yet?" asked one of the two young women whose acquaintance Blake and Joe had made through the courtesy of Captain Merceau.

"Oh, yes," Blake answered. "We have been for some time."

"But I thought when we got there we would be protected by warships or torpedo-boat destroyers," said Miss Hanson.

"We're supposed to be," replied Joe. "I've been looking for a sight of one. They may be along any minute. Look, there comes a messenger from the wireless room. He's going to the bridge where the captain is. Maybe that's word from a destroyer now."

Interestedly they watched the messenger make his way to the bridge with a slip of paper in his hand. And then, before he could reach it, there came a hail from the lookout in the crow's nest high above the deck.

He called in French, but Joe and Blake knew what he said. It was:

"Periscope ahoy! Two points off on the port bow! Periscope ahoy!"

CHAPTER VIII

BEATEN OFF

Decks that, a moment, before, had exhibited scenes of quietness, though there was a nervous tenseness on all sides, at once assumed feverish activity. Officers on duty, hearing the cry of the lookout, called to him to repeat his message, which he did, with the added information that the submarine, as evidenced by the appearance of the periscope cutting the water, was approaching nearer, and with great swiftness.

"Here she comes, Blake!" cried Joe, as the two boys stood together at the spot from which they had been watching the wireless messenger a moment before. "Here she comes! Now for a chance at a picture!"

"You're not going below, are you?" cried Blake.

"Why not?" asked Joe, pausing on his way to the companionway.

"Why, we may be blown up at any moment! We may be hit by a torpedo! I don't see why they haven't loosed one at us before this, as their periscope is in sight. You shouldn't go below now! Stay on deck, where you'll have a chance to get in the boat you're assigned to!"

"I've got to go below to get the small camera," answered Joe. "I ought to have kept it on deck. I'm going to, after this, to have it ready."

"But, Joe, the torpedo may be on its way now - under water!"

"That's just what I want to get a picture of! I guess if we're going to be blown up, being below deck or on deck doesn't make much difference. I want to get that picture!"

And, seeing that his chum was very much in earnest, Blake, not to let Joe do it alone, went below with him to get the camera. But on the way they met Charlie coming up with it.

"She's all loaded, boys, ready for action!" cried the lanky Macaroni. "I started down for it as soon as I heard the lookout yell! I didn't know what he was jabbering about, seeing I don't understand much French, but I guessed it was a submarine. Am I right?"

"Yes!" shouted Joe. "Good work, Mac! Now for a picture!"

And while Joe and his two friends were thus making ready, in the face of imminent disaster, to get pictures of the torpedo that might be on its way to sink the ship, many other matters were being undertaken.

Passengers were being called to take the places previously assigned to them in the lifeboats. Captain Merceau and his officers, after a hasty consultation, were gathered on the bridge, looking for the first sight of the submarine, or, what was more vital, for the ripples that would disclose the presence of the torpedo.

But perhaps the most eager of all, and certainly among the most active, were the members of the gun crews. On both sides of the vessel, and at bow and stern, the call to quarters had been answered promptly, and with strained but eager eyes the young men, under their lieutenants, were watching for the first fair sight of something at which to loose the missiles of the quick-firing guns.

"Give it to her, lads! Give it to her! All you can pump in!" yelled the commander of the squad on the port side, for it was off that bow that the lookout had sighted the periscope.

And while the hurried preparations went on for getting the passengers into the lifeboats, at the falls of which the members of the crew stood ready to lower away, there came from the port gun a rattle and barking of fire.

The periscope had disappeared for a moment after the lookout had sighted it, but a slight disturbance in the water, a ripple that was different from the line of foam caused by the breaking waves, showed where it had been.

And by the time Joe and Blake, with the help of Charlie, had set up their small camera, the tell-tale indicator of an undersea boat was again in view, coming straight for the steamer.

"There she is!" cried Blake.

"I see her!" answered Joe, as he focussed the lens of

the machine on the object "I'll get her as soon as she breaks!"

The mewing picture boys, as well as Charlie, had forgotten all about the need of taking their places at the stations assigned to them, to be in readiness to get into a boat. They were sharply reminded of this by one of the junior officers.

"Take your places! Take your places!" he cried.

"Not yet!" answered Joe. "We want to get a shot at her first!"

"But, young gentlemen, you must not shoot with that. It will be ineffectual! Let the gunners do their work, I beg of you. Take your places at the boats!"

"That's all right!" exclaimed Blake "We're only going to shoot some moving pictures."

"Ah, what brave rashness!" murmured the French officer, as he hurried away.

Blake and Joe, with Charlie to steady the machine, for the steamer was now zigzagging at high speed in an effort to escape the expected torpedo, were taking pictures of the approach of the submarine. The underwater craft was still coming on, her periscope in the midst of a hail of fire from the steamer's guns. For, now that the vessel was making turns, it was possible for two gun crews, alternately, to fire at the German boat.

"There goes the periscope!" yelled Charlie, as a burst of shots, concentrated on the brass tube, seemed to dispose of it.

But he had spoken too soon. The submarine had merely drawn the periscope within herself, it being of the telescope variety, and the next moment, with a movement of the water as if some monster leviathan were breaking from the ocean depths, the steel-plated and rivet-studded back of the submarine rose, glistening in the sun and in full view of those on deck, not two hundred yards away.

"There she blows!" cried Charlie, as an old salt might announce the presence of a whale. "There she blows! Film her, boys!"

And Blake and Joe were doing just that.

Meanwhile even wilder excitement, if possible, prevailed on deck. There was a rush for the boats that nearly overwhelmed the crews stationed to lower them from the sides, and the officers had all they could do to preserve order.

"The torpedo! The torpedo at the stern!" cried the lookout, who, notwithstanding his position of almost certain death should the ship be struck, had not deserted his elevated post. "They have loosed a torpedo at the stern!"

Blake and Joe, who were well aft, looked for a moment away from the submarine, and saw a line of bubbles approaching the stern and a ripple that indicated the presence of that dread engine of war - an air-driven torpedo.

And as if the ship herself knew what doom awaited her

should the torpedo so much as touch her, she increased her speed, and to such good purpose that the mass of gun-cotton, contained in the steel cylinder that had been launched from the submarine, passed under the stern. But only a few feet from the rudder did it pass. By such a little margin was the ship saved.

And then, having a broader mark at which to aim, the gunners sent a perfect hail of lead and shells at the underwater boat, and with such effect that some hits were made. Whether or not they were vital ones it was impossible to learn, for there was a sudden motion to the submarine, which had been quietly resting on the surface for a moment, and then she slipped beneath the waves again.

"Driven off!" cried Blake, as he and Joe got the final pictures of this drama - a drama that had come so near being a tragedy. "They've beaten her off!"

"But we're not safe yet!" cried Charlie. "She may shoot another torpedo at us from under water - she can do that, all right! Look out, boys!"

There was need of this, yet it was impossible to do more toward saving one's life than to take to the boats. And even that, under the inhuman and ruthless system of the Huns, was no guarantee that one would be saved. Lifeboats had, more than once, been shelled by Germans.

The appearance of the submarine had added to the panic caused by the sight of the periscope, and there was a rush for the boats that took all the power and authority of the officers to manage it.

There was a period of anxious waiting, but either the submarine had no other torpedoes, or, if she did fire any, they went wide, or, again, the gunfire from the vessel may have disabled her entirely. She did not again show herself above the surface. Even the periscope was not observed.

Having nothing to picture, Blake and Joe turned away from the camera for a moment. Some of the lifeboats had already been filled with their loads when Charlie, pointing to something afar off, cried:

"Here comes another boat!"

On the horizon a dense cloud of black smoke showed.

CHAPTER IX

SUSPICIONS

For a moment there was more terror and excitement aboard the *Jeanne*, if it were possible, after it became certain that another craft, the nature of which none knew, was headed toward the French steamer. Then an officer gifted with sound common-sense, cried out in English, so that the majority could understand:

"It is a destroyer! It is a destroyer belonging to the Stars and Stripes coming to our rescue. Three cheers!"

Nobody gave the three cheers, but it heartened every one to hear them called for, and the real meaning of the smoke was borne to all.

"Of course it can't be a submarine!" exclaimed Blake. "They don't send out any smoke, and there aren't any other German boats at sea. It's a destroyer!"

"One of ours, do you think?" asked Charlie.

"Perhaps. Uncle Sam has a lot of 'em over here to act as convoys. Probably this is our escort coming up a little late to the ball," said Joe.

"But we did very well by ourselves," observed Blake.

"It was a narrow squeak, though."

And indeed it was a narrow escape. The *Jeanne* had, unaided, driven off the undersea boat, and perhaps had damaged her by the rain of shot and shell poured at her steel sides. They could not feel sure of this, though, for the approach of the destroyer was probably known to the submarine, for they have underwater telephones which tell them, by means of the throbbing of the screws and propellers in the water, just about how far away another ship is, and what speed she is making, as well as the direction from which she is coming.

Whether the submarine had expended her last torpedo, or whether having missed what she intended for a vital shot she deemed there was not time to launch another and had sunk out of sight, or whether she were disabled, were questions perhaps never to be answered.

At any rate, the approach of the destroyer, which came on with amazing speed, served to make the *Jeanne* comparatively safe. The lifeboats were emptied of their passengers, and once more there was a feeling of comparative safety as the passengers again thronged the decks.

On came the destroyer. She proved to be one of Uncle Sam's boats, and the joy with which she was greeted was vociferous and perhaps a little hysterical. She had learned by wireless of the appearance of the French craft in the danger zone, and had come to fulfill her mission. She had been delayed by a slight accident, or she would have been on hand when the submarine first approached.

The wireless message that had come just as the

German craft appeared had been from the destroyer, to bid those aboard the *Jeanne* have no fear, for help was on the way. And soon after the grim and swift craft from the United States had begun to slide along beside the *Jeanne* two more destroyers, one of them British, made their appearance, coming up with the speed of ocean greyhounds.

There was great rejoicing among the passengers, and much credit was given the lookout for his promptness in reporting a sight of the submarine. Formal thanks were extended to the gun crews for their efficient work, without which the undersea boat might have accomplished her purpose. Nor were the boiler room and engineer forces forgotten, for it was because of the sudden burst of speed on the part of the *Jeanne* that she escaped that one torpedo at least.

"Now we'll be all right," Charlie said, as he helped his friends make a few pictures of the approach and the convoying of the destroyers to add to the views they had of the submarine and her defeat - temporary defeat it might prove, but, none the less, a defeat.

"Well, hardly all right," remarked Blake, as the camera was dismounted. "We're still in the danger zone, and the Huns won't let slip any chance to do us harm. But I guess we have more of a chance for our white alley than we had before."

Though the French ship was now protected by the three convoying vessels, the crews of which kept a sharp watch on all sides for the presence of more submarines, there was still plenty of danger, and this was felt by all.

At any moment a submarine, approaching below the surface with only her periscope showing - and this made a mark exceedingly hard to see and hit - might launch a torpedo, not only at the merchant-man but at one of the destroyers.

"It's like sleeping over a case of dynamite," observed Joe, as he and his chums went below. "I'd rather be on the war front. You can at least see and hear shells coming."

"That's right," agreed Blake. "Well, if nothing happens, we'll soon be there now."

"*If* is a big word these days," observed Charlie.

"Now that we're comparatively safe for the moment, I want to ask you fellows something," said Blake, after a pause.

"Ask ahead," returned Joe. "If you want to know whether I was scared, I'll say I was, but I was too busy getting pictures to notice it. If it is something else -"

"It is," interrupted Blake, and his manner was grave. "Come below and I'll tell you. I don't want any one else to hear."

Wondering somewhat at their friend's manner, Joe and Charlie went to their stateroom, and there Blake closed the door and took the dark cloth down from the mirror. A look into it showed that the transom of the room opposite - the cabin of Levi Labenstein - had been closed.

"So we can't tell whether he's in there or not," said Blake.

"Did you want to talk about him?" asked Joe.

"Yes, him and the lieutenant. Did you fellows happen to notice what they were doing when the submarine was attacking us?"

"Not especially," answered Joe. "I did see Lieutenant Secor looking at us as we worked the camera, but I didn't pay much attention to him."

"It wasn't him so much as it was the German," went on Blake.

"In what way?"

"Did you see where he was standing when the submarine came out of the water?"

Neither Joe nor Charlie had done so, or, if they had, they did not recall the matter when Blake questioned them. So that young man resumed:

"Well, I'll tell you what I saw: Labenstein was leaning over the rail on the side where the submarine showed, and he was holding a big white cloth over the side."

"A big white cloth?" cried Joe.

"That's what it was," went on Blake. "It looked to me like a signal."

"Do you mean a signal of surrender?" asked Charlie. "A white flag? He wouldn't have any right to display that, anyhow. It would have to come from Captain Merceau."

"Maybe he meant that he'd surrender personally," suggested Joe, "and didn't want his fellow-murderers to hurt him."

"I don't know what his object was," went on Blake, "but I saw him take from his pocket a big white cloth and hold it over the side. It could easily have been seen from the submarine, and must have been, for he displayed it just before the underwater boat came up."

"A white cloth," mused Joe. "From his pocket. Was it his handkerchief, Blake?"

"He wouldn't have one as large as that, even if he suffered from hay fever. I think it was a signal."

"A signal for what?" Charlie again asked.

"To tell the submarine some piece of news, of course - perhaps the port of sailing, something of the nature of our cargo, or perhaps to tell just where to send the torpedo. I understand we are carrying some munitions, and it may be that this German spy directed the commander of the sub-marine where to aim the torpedo so as to explode them."

"But he'd be signaling for his own death warrant!" cried Joe.

"Not necessarily," answered Blake. "He may have had some understanding with the submarine that he was to be saved first. Perhaps he was going to jump overboard before the torpedo was fired and was to be picked up. Anyhow, I saw him draping a white cloth over the side, and I'm sure it was a signal."

"Well, I guess you're right," said Joe. "The next question is, what's to be done? This fellow is a spy and a traitor, and we ought to expose him."

"Yes," agreed Blake. "But we'd better have a little more evidence than just my word. You fellows didn't see what I saw, that's plain, and perhaps no one else did. So it would only make a big fuss and not result in anything if I told the captain."

"Then what are you going to do?" asked Charlie.

"Just keep watch," Blake answered.

"What about Lieutenant Secor?" asked Joe.

"Well, I didn't see him do anything," admitted Blake. "Though I have my suspicions of him also. He and Labenstein weren't talking so earnestly together for nothing. We'll watch that Frenchman, too."

"And if he tries any more games in spoiling films I'll have my say!" threatened Macaroni.

The boys talked the situation over at some length as they put away the films they had taken of the submarine attack, and agreed that "watchful waiting" was the best policy to adopt. As Blake had said, little could be gained by denouncing Labenstein with only the word of one witness to rely on.

"If all three of us catch him at his traitorous work, then we'll denounce him," suggested Blake.

"Yes, and the Frenchman, too!" added Charlie, in a louder voice, so that Blake raised a cautioning hand.

At that moment came a knock on their door, and a voice said:

"I am Mr. Labenstein!"

CHAPTER X

THE FLASHLIGHT

Almost like conspirators themselves, the boys looked at one another as the voice and knock sounded together. Blake was the first to recover himself.

"Come in!" he called, in as welcoming a tone as he could muster under the circumstances. Then as the knob of the door was ineffectually tried, he added:

"Oh, I forgot it was locked! Wait a moment!"

A moment later he had swung the door open, and the man who, the boys believed, was a German spy confronted them, smiling.

"You are locked in as if you feared another submarine," he said. "It is not the best way to do. You should be on deck!"

"But not on deck as you were, with a flag to signal to the Huns," thought Joe; and he wished he dared make the accusation.

Blake motioned to the caller to seat himself on a stool.

"I came to see if I might borrow something," began the

caller. "I find that mine is out of order for some reason," and he held out a small, but powerful, electric flash lamp, of the sort sold for the use of soldiers. "Have you, by any chance, one that you could spare me?" asked Mr. Labenstein.

"I do not want it, if it is the only one you have, but they are a great convenience in one's berth, for the lights must be kept turned off, now that we are in the danger zone made by those terrible Germans. Ah, how I hate them!" and his anger seemed very real and earnest.

"Did you say you wanted to borrow a pocket electric flash lamp?" asked Blake, wishing to make the caller repeat his request. As he asked this question Blake looked at his chums, as though to ask them to take particular note of the reply.

"I should like to, yes, if you have one to spare. There are three of you, and, I presume, like most travelers, you each have one. I am alone in a single stateroom, and I may have need of a light. I will return it to you at the end of the voyage, or buy it of you at a good price. You see, I have a little Jew in me. I will make a bargain with you. And I will pay you well, something a Jew proverbially does not like to do. But I realize the value of what I want, and that the market is not well supplied, so you may take advantage of my situation. My battery is either worn out or the light is broken. It will not flash."

He shoved down the little sliding catch, but there was no glow in the tiny tungsten bulb.

"You have me at your mercy if you wish to sell me a lamp," he went on, with a smile and a shrug of his shoulders, not unlike that of Lieutenant Secor.

"Hasn't your friend a spare light?" asked Joe quickly.

"My friend?" repeated the German, as though surprised. "You mean -?"

"I mean Lieutenant Secor."

"Oh, him!" and again came the deprecatory shrug of the shoulders. "He is an acquaintance, not a friend. Besides, he has but one lamp, and he needs that. So, also, will you need yours. But as there are three of you together, I thought perhaps -"

"We each have a light," said Blake, interrupting the rather rapid talk of Labenstein. "In fact, I have two, and I'll let you take one."

"That is very kind of you. Ah, it is like mine!"

The visitor was watching Blake eagerly as he brought forth one of the flat, three-cell nickel-plated holders of tiny batteries, with the white-backed and tungsten-filamented incandescent light set in a depressed socket.

"Yes, this is the best type," Blake said. "You may have this."

"And the price?" asked Labenstein, as his hand quickly went into his pocket.

"Is nothing," answered Blake. "It is a gift."

"Ah, but, my dear sir, that is too much! I could not think of taking it without pay!" insisted Mr.

Labenstein, as he flashed on the light and then slipped the switch back in place again. "I protest that I must pay you."

"Please don't insist on paying," begged Blake, "for I shall only have to refuse to take any money. Please consider the light a gift. I have a spare one."

"You are very kind, I'm sure," said the other, bowing with some exaggeration, it seemed to the boys. "I appreciate it, I assure you, and I shall look for a chance to repay the favor."

"That's all right," said Blake, and he tried to make his voice sound hearty. "You are welcome to the light."

"A thousand thanks," murmured Mr. Labenstein, as he bowed himself out.

And then, when the door had closed on him and they had taken the precaution of closing their transom, Joe burst out in a cautious whisper with:

"What in the world did you let him take it for, Blake Stewart? Don't you see what his game is?"

"Yes," was Blake's quiet answer; "I think I do."

"Well, then -"

"What is his game?" asked Charlie.

"I presume he wants to use the flash lamp to give a signal at night to some German submarine," said Blake quietly - very quietly, under the circumstances, it might seem.

"And you let him take a light for that?" cried Joe.

"Wait a bit!" advised Blake, and he smiled at his chum. "Do you know anything about these flashlights, Joe?"

"A little - yes. I know a powerful one, like that you gave Labenstein, can be seen a long way on a dark night."

"Well, then maybe you know something else about them, or you may have forgotten it. Like the proverb which says 'blessings brighten as they vanish,' so the light of these lamps sometimes glows very strong just before the battery goes on the blink and douses the glim."

Joe looked at his chum for a moment, uncomprehendingly, and then a smile came over his face.

"Do you mean you gave him a light with a battery in it that was almost played out?" he asked.

"Exactly," answered Blake, with another smile. "This is a light I have had for some time. I noticed, only last night, that it was brighter than usual. Just as a fountain pen - at least, the old-fashioned kind - used to flow more freely when there were only a few drops of ink left, so this battery seems to be strongest just before it gives out altogether.

"I suspected this was going to happen, but I tested the battery with a galvanometer to-day and I found out it has about ten flashes left. After that the light will be dead."

"Is that why you gave it to him?" asked Charlie.

"The very reason. As soon as he asked for a light it occurred to me that he wanted to use it - or might use it - to give a signal at night to some watching submarine commander waiting for a chance to torpedo us. I thought if I let him do it with this failing light he might do the Huns more damage than he could us."

"How?" asked Joe.

"By not being able to give the proper signals. He'll need to flash a light for some little time to make sure to attract the attention of the submarine, won't he?"

"Probably," agreed Joe.

"Well, then, if, while he's in the midst of signaling, his light goes out, the submarine won't know what to make of it, and will come up closer to find out what's wrong. Then our own guns, or those of the destroyers, can bang away and catch the Germans napping."

"Say, that's great!" cried Charlie, as soon as he understood the plan Blake had so quickly evolved.

"If it works," conceded Joe. "But how are we going to know when that German spy signals the submarine and fails to convey his full meaning, Blake?"

"We'll have to watch him, of course. Catch him in the act, as it were. The defective lamp will help."

"So it will!" exclaimed Joe. "Blake, I take back all I thought of you. I imagined you were making a mistake to let that lamp go out of your possession; but now I see your game. It's a good one! But we've got to be on the watch for this spy!"

"Oh, yes," agreed his chum. "And not only him but the Frenchman as well. I didn't believe it possible that Secor could be in with this German, but perhaps he is, and maybe he'll betray his own countrymen. Either one may give the signal, but if they do we'll be ready for them. No more moving pictures for us, boys, until we get to the war front. We've got to be on this other job!"

"But hadn't we better tell Captain Merceau?" asked Charlie.

"Yes, I think so," assented Blake. "We'll tell him what we think, and what we have done."

But they did not get a chance that day, for there was a submarine scare toward evening - a lookout thinking he saw a periscope - and the consequent confusion made it impossible to have a talk with the commander. The boys did not want to report to any subordinate officer, and so concluded to wait until the next day.

"But we'll keep watch to-night on our friend across the corridor," Blake said. "And on Lieutenant Secor as well. His stateroom is next to Labenstein's, and we can tell when either of them goes out after dark - that is, if we keep watch."

"And we'll keep it, all right!" declared Joe "Now that we know something about what to look out for, we'll do it!"

And so, as evening came on and the lights of the ship were darkened and as she sped along in company with her convoy, the three boys prepared to divide the night into watches, that they might be on guard against what they regarded as an attempt at black treachery.

For somewhere under or on that waste of waters they believed a deadly submarine was lurking, awaiting the favorable moment to send a torpedo at the ship.

CHAPTER XI

THE DEPTH CHARGE

Charlie Anderson, who had taken the earliest watch, roused Blake at the appointed time, and reported:

"All quiet so far."

"Then you haven't seen anything of our friends across the hall?"

"Not a thing. Just as we arranged, I've had my eye at the hole, but their doors have both been closed. Maybe you'll have better luck."

"I don't think it will be good luck at all to see one of them sneak out to flash a signal to a waiting submarine, or one that may be following us all the while, waiting for a chance to strike. But I will call it exceedingly good luck if we can stop it," said Blake.

"Go to it, old top!" exclaimed Macaroni, dropping into what he thought the latest English slang. "I'm going to turn in."

The lanky helper of the moving picture boys had spent the hours of his watch with his eye close to a small hole that had been bored in the door of the boys' stateroom. The hole gave a view of the staterooms of Lieutenant Secor and Mr. Labenstein, which adjoined. And, as Charles had said, he had not observed either man leave his apartment.

If what the boys had only guessed at were true - that one or both of the men contemplated giving a signal to the enemy by means of the flashlight - the time for it had not yet come.

"Well, I'll try my hand," Blake said. "You turn in, Mac, and if I need any help I'll call you. If I don't see anything up to about one o'clock I'll let Joe do his trick. Good-night and pleasant dreams."

Charlie did not answer. He was already in his bunk and asleep, for he was tired, and the last half hour of his watch he had kept himself awake with difficulty.

Then Blake began his turn of duty. He took a position at the door where he could look out through the hole into the dimly lighted corridor. He had a view of the doors of the staterooms of the two men who were under suspicion, and as soon as either or both of them came out he intended to follow and see what was done.

For an hour nothing happened, and Blake was beginning to feel a bit sleepy, in spite of the fact that he had rested during the early part of the evening, when he was startled by a slight sound. It was like the creaking of a rusty hinge, and at first he thought it but one of the many sounds always more or less audible on a moving ship.

Then, as he tuned his ears more acutely, he knew that it was the squeaking of a hinge he had heard, and he felt sure it meant the opening of a door near by.

Through the hole he looked at the door behind which was Levi Labenstein, whether sleeping or preparing for some act which would put the ship in peril and endanger the lives of all the passengers, could only be guessed.

Then, as Blake watched, he saw the door open and the German come out. Labenstein looked around with furtive glances, and they rested for some little time on the door behind which Blake was watching. Then, as if satisfied that all was quiet, the man stole silently along, the corridor.

"Something doing," thought Blake. "Something doing, all right. He has something in his hand - probably my flashlight. Much good may it do him!"

As Labenstein passed the stateroom where Lieutenant Secor was quartered, that door opened softly, but not until the German was beyond it. And then Blake saw the Frenchman peer out as though to make sure his fellow-conspirator was fairly on his way. After that the lieutenant himself emerged and softly followed the German.

"Both of 'em at it," mused Blake. "I'd better rouse Joe and let him keep track of one, in case they should separate."

A touch on Joe Duncan's shoulder served to arouse him, though he was in a deep sleep. He sat up, demanding:

"What is it? Are we torpedoed?"

"No, but we may be," was Blake's low answer. "Keep quiet and follow me. Secor and Labenstein have both gone up on deck, I think. We'd better follow."

"Shall we tell Charlie?" asked Joe, as he slid from his berth. Neither he nor his chums had taken off their clothes.

"Yes, I guess we'd better get him up," Blake answered. "If you and I have to watch these two fellows, we may need some one to send for help in case anything happens. Come on, Macaroni," he added, leaning over their helper and whispering in his ear. "Wake up!"

Charles was up in an instant, a bit confused at first, as one often is when emerging from a heavy sleep, but he had his faculties with him almost at once, and was ready for action.

"What is it?" he asked, in a whisper.

In like low tones Blake told him, and then the three boys, after making sure by a cautious observation that neither of the suspected men was in sight, went out into the corridor and to the deck.

It was quite dark, for all unnecessary lights were dimmed, but there was a new moon, and the stars were bright, so that objects were fairly clear. On either side could be dimly observed the black shapes of the convoying destroyers.

"Where are they?" asked Joe, in a whisper. "The traitors!"

"I don't know - we'll have to look," was Blake's

answer. They looked along the deck, but saw no one, and were about to turn to the other end of the craft when a figure stepped out from the shadow of a boat and sharply challenged them.

"Who are you - what do you want?" was asked.

It was one of the ship's crew assigned to night-watch. Blake knew him slightly, having, at the man's request one day, showed him something of the workings of a moving picture camera.

"We came up looking for two gentlemen who have the staterooms opposite ours," Blake answered, resolving to "take a chance" in the matter. "Lieutenant Secor and Mr. Labenstein," he added. "Have you seen them?"

"Yes; they came up to get a bit of air, they said," answered the sailor. "I saw them a little while ago. You will find them up near the bow. Do not show a light, whatever you do, and light no matches. If you wish to smoke you must go below."

"Thanks, we don't smoke," Joe answered, with a low laugh. "But we'll be careful about lights."

"All right," answered the sailor. "We have to look out for submarines, you know," he added. "This is the worst part of the danger zone."

The boys moved forward like silent shadows, peering here and there for a sight of the two figures who had come up a little while before them, with evil intentions in their hearts they had no doubt. Even now there might be flashing across the dark sea, from some hidden vantage point on the ship, a light signal that would mean the launching of the deadly torpedo.

"There's no doubt, now, but the Frenchman is a traitor," whispered Joe to Blake. "I have been positive about that German being a spy ever since I've seen him, but I did have some doubts regarding Secor. I haven't any now."

"It does look bad," admitted Blake.

"I wish I'd smashed him with my auto, instead of waiting for him to smash me," remarked Charlie. "He's a snake, that's what he is!"

"Hush!" cautioned Blake. "They may be around here - any place - and hear you. I wish we could see them."

They moved along silently, looking on every side for a sight of the two conspirators, but there were so many shadows, and so many places where the men might lurk, that it was difficult to place them. The sailor, evidently, had had no suspicions, thinking that Blake and his chums had merely come up to be with the two men.

"What are you going to do when you do see them?" asked Joe of his chum.

"I don't know," was the whispered answer. "First, we've got to see them, then we can tell what to do. But where in the world are they?"

Somewhat at a loss what to do, the boys paused in the shadow of a deckhouse. They were about to emerge from its dim protection when Charlie plucked at Blake's sleeve.

"Well?" asked the moving picture boy, in a low voice. "What is it?"

"Look right straight into the bow, as far as you can see," directed Macaroni. "Notice those two moving shadows?"

"Yes," answered Blake.

"I think that's our men," went on Charlie.

"Yes, there they are," added Joe.

It was evident, after a moment's glance, that the two men who had so silently stolen from their rooms were together in the bow of the steamer, or as far up in the bow as they could get. The deck was open at this point, and, leaning over the side, it would be easy to flash a signal on either beam. The lookout on the bridge was probably too much occupied in sweeping the sea ahead and to either side of the ship to direct his attention to the vessel itself.

"Come on," whispered Blake to the other two. "We want to hear what they are saying if we can, and see what they're doing."

Silently the boys stole forward until they could make out the dim figures more clearly. There was no doubt that they were those of Secor and Labenstein. And then, as the boys paused, fearing to get so close as to court discovery, they saw a little light flash.

Three times up and down on the port side of the bows went a little flash of light, and then it suddenly went out.

"My electric light," whispered Blake in Joe's ear.

"But I thought you said it would burn out!"

"I hope it has. I think -"

From one of the figures in the bow came a guttural exclamation:

"The infernal light has gone out!"

"So?" came from the other.

"Yes. It must be broken. Let me have yours, Herr Lieutenant. I have not given the signal in completeness, and -"

"I left my light in the stateroom. I'll go and -"

But the lieutenant never finished that sentence. Across the dark and silent ocean came a dull report - an explosion that seemed to make the *Jeanne* tremble. And then the sky and the water was lighted by the flashing beams of powerful lights.

"What was that?" gasped Joe, while from the crouching figures in the bow came exclamations of dismay. "Are we torpedoed?"

"I fancy not," answered Blake. "Sounded more like one of the destroyers made a hit herself. I think they set off a depth charge against a submarine. We'll soon know! Look at the lights now!"

The sea was agleam with brilliant radiance.

CHAPTER XII

IN ENGLAND

From the bridge came commands to the lookouts stationed in various parts of the French steamer. Orders flashed to the engine room, and the vessel lost way and floated under her momentum. As yet she was shrouded in darkness, the only lights glowing being those actually required to enable persons to see their way about. Below, of course, as long as the incandescents were shaded, they could be turned on, and many passengers, awakened by the concussion and the following sounds, illuminated their staterooms.

The lights that gleamed across the billows came from the convoying destroyers, and signals flashed from one to the other, though the meaning of them the moving picture boys could only guess at.

Immediately following the explosion, which seemed to come from the side of the *Jeanne* where Labenstein had flashed his signal, the German and the Frenchman had subsided into silence. Each one had given voice to an exclamation in his own tongue and then had hurried away.

And so occupied were Blake and his chums with what had gone on out there on the ocean - trying to guess what had happened - that they did not notice the departure of the two men.

"What's that you said it was?" asked Joe of his partner. "I mean the explosion."

"I think it was a depth charge," answered Blake. "One of the destroyers must have sighted a submarine and let go a bomb, with a heavy charge of explosive, which didn't go off until after it got to a certain depth below the surface. That's the new way of dealing with submarines, you know."

"I only hope they got this one, with a depth charge or any other way," remarked Charles Anderson. "Look, we're lighting up! I guess the danger must be over."

Lights were flashing on the deck of the *Jeanne*, and signals came from the destroyers. It was evident that messages were being sent to and fro.

And then, as passengers crowded up from their staterooms, some in a state of panic fearing a torpedo had been launched at the ship, another muffled explosion was heard, and in the glare of the searchlights from one of the convoying ships a column of water could be seen spurting up between the French steamer and the war vessel.

"That's caused by a depth charge," Blake announced. "They must be making sure of the submarine."

"If they haven't, we're a good target for her now," said Joe, as he noted the lights agleam on their steamer. "They're taking an awful chance, it seems to me."

"I guess the captain knows what he's doing," stated Blake. "He must have been signaled from the destroyers. We'll try to find out."

An officer went about among the passengers, calming them and telling them there was no danger now.

"But what happened?" asked Blake, and he and his chums waited eagerly for an answer.

"It was a submarine," was the officer's reply. "She came to attack us, trying to slip around or between our convoying ships. But one of the lookouts sighted her and depth charges were fired. The submarine came up, disabled, it seemed, but to make sure another charge was exploded beneath the surface. And that was the end of the Hun!" he cried.

"Good!" exclaimed Blake, and his chums also rejoiced. There was rejoicing, too, among the other passengers, for they had escaped death by almost as narrow a margin as before. Only the sharp lookout kept had saved them - that and the depth charge.

"But how does that depth charge work?" asked Charlie Anderson, when the chums were back in their cabin again, discussing what they had better do in reference to telling the captain of the conduct of Labenstein and Secor.

"It works on the principle that water is incompressible in any and all directions," answered Blake. "That is, pressure exerted on a body of water is transmitted in all directions by the water. Thus, if you push suddenly on top of a column of water the water rises.

"And if you set off an explosive below the surface of water the force goes up, down sidewise and in all directions. In fact, if you explode gun-cotton near a vessel below the surface it does more damage than if set off nearer to her but on the surface. The water transmits the power.

"A depth charge is a bomb timed to go off at a certain depth. If it explodes anywhere near a submarine, it blows in her plates and she is done for. That's what happened this time, I imagine."

And that is exactly what had happened, as nearly as could be told by the observers on the destroyer. The submarine had risen, only to sink disabled with all on board. A few pieces of wreckage and a quantity of oil floated to the surface but that was all.

Once more the *Jeanne* resumed her way in the midst of the protecting convoys, the value of which had been amply demonstrated. And when all was once more quiet on board, Blake and his chums resumed their talk about what was best to do regarding what they had observed just before the setting off of the depth charge.

"I think we ought to tell the captain," said Charlie.

"So do I," added Joe.

"And I agree with the majority," said Blake. "Captain Merceau shall be informed."

The commander was greatly astonished when told what the boys had seen. He questioned them at length, and made sure there could have been no mistake.

"And they gave a signal," mused the captain. "It hardly seems possible!"

"It was Labenstein who actually flashed the light," said Blake. "Do you know anything about him, Captain Merceau?"

"Nothing more than that his papers, passport, and so on are in proper shape. He is a citizen of your own country, and appeared to be all right, or he would not have been permitted to take passage with us. I am astounded!"

"What about the Frenchman?" asked Joe.

"Him I know," declared the captain. "Not well, but enough to say that I would have ventured everything on his honor. It does not seem possible that he can be a traitor!"

"And yet we saw him with the German while Labenstein was signaling the submarine," added Blake.

"Yes, I suppose it must be so. I am sorry! It is a blot on the fair name of France that one of her sons should so act! But we must be careful. It is not absolute proof, yet. They could claim that they were only on deck to smoke, or something like that. To insure punishment, we must have absolute proof. I thank you young gentlemen. From now on these two shall be under strict surveillance, and when we reach England I shall inform the authorities. You have done your duty. I will now be responsible for these men."

"That relieves us," said Blake. "We shan't stay in England long ourselves, so if you want our testimony you'd better arrange to have it taken soon after we land."

"I shall; and thank you! This is terrible!"

The boys realized that, as the captain had said, adequate proof would be required to cause the arrest and conviction of the two plotters. While it was morally certain that they had tried to bring about the successful attack on the French steamer, a court would want undisputed evidence to pronounce sentence, whether of death or imprisonment.

"I guess we'll have to leave it with the captain," decided Blake. "We can tell of his borrowing the light, and that we saw him flash it. Of course he can say we saw only his lighted cigarette, or something like that, and where would we be?"

"But there was the signal with the white cloth," added Joe.

"Yes, we could tell that, too; but it isn't positive."

"And there was Secor's running into me and spoiling our other films," said Charlie.

"That, too, would hardly be enough," went on Blake. "What the authorities will have to do will be to search the baggage of these fellows, and see if there is anything incriminating among their papers. We can't do that, so we'll have to wait."

And wait they did. In spite of what Captain Merceau had said, the boys did not relax their vigilance, but though, to their minds, the two men acted suspiciously, there was nothing definite that could be fastened on them.

Watchful guard was maintained night and day against an attack by submarines, and though there were several alarms, they turned out to be false. And in due season, the vessel arrived at "an English port," as the papers stated.

"Let's go and see if Captain Merceau wants us to give any evidence against those fellows," suggested Joe; and this seemed a good plan to follow.

"Ah, yes, my American friends!" the commander murmured, as the boys were shown into his cabin. "What can I do for you?"

"We thought we'd see if you wanted us in relation to the arrest of Secor and Labenstein," answered Blake.

"Ah, yes! The two men who signaled the submarine. I have had them under surveillance ever since you made your most startling disclosures. I sent a wireless to the war authorities here to come and place them under arrest as soon as the vessel docked. I have no doubt they are in custody now. I'll send and see."

He dispatched a messenger who, when he returned, held a rapid conversation with the captain in French. It was evident that something unusual had taken place.

The captain grew more excited, and finally, turning to the boys, said in English, which he spoke fluently:

"I regret to tell you there has been a mistake."

"A mistake!" cried Blake.

"Yes. Owing to some error, those men were released before the war authorities could apprehend them. They have gone ashore!"

CHAPTER XIII

UNDER SUSPICION

Blake, Joe and Charles looked at one another. Then they glanced at Captain Merceau. For one wild moment Blake had it in mind to suspect the commander; but a look at his face, which showed plainly how deeply chagrined he was at the failure to keep the two under surveillance, told the young moving picture operator that there was no ground for his thought.

"They got away!" repeated Joe, as though he could hardly believe it.

"Yes, I regret to say that is what my officer reports to me. It is too bad; but I will at once send out word, and they may be traced and apprehended. I'll at once send word to the authorities." This he did by the same messenger who had brought the intelligence that the Frenchman and the German had secretly left.

When this had been done, and the boys had got themselves ready to go ashore and report, Captain Merceau told them how it had happened. He had given orders, following the report made by Blake and his chums, that Secor and Labenstein should be kept under careful watch. And this was to be done without allowing them to become aware of it.

"However, I very much doubt if this was the case," the captain frankly admitted. "They are such scoundrels themselves that they would naturally suspect others of suspecting them. So they must have become aware of our plans, and then they made arrangements to elude the guard I set over them."

"How did they do that?" asked Blake.

"By a trick. One of them pretended to be ill and asked that the surgeon be summoned. This was the German. And when the guard hurried away on what he supposed was an errand of mercy, the two rascals slipped away. They were soon lost in the crowd. But we shall have them back, have no fear, young gentlemen."

But, all the same, Blake and his chums had grave doubts as to the ability of the authorities to capture the two men. Not that they had any fears for themselves, for, as Joe said, they had nothing to apprehend personally from the men.

"Unless they are after the new films we take," suggested Charles.

"Why should they want them?" asked Blake. "I mean, our films are not likely to give away any vital secrets," he went on.

"Well, I don't know," answered the lanky helper, "but I have a sort of hunch that they'll do all they can and everything they can to spoil our work for Uncle Sam on this side of the water, as they did before."

"Secor spoiled the films before," urged Blake. "He

didn't know Labenstein then, as far as we know."

"Well, he knows him now," said Charles. "I'm going to be on the watch."

"I guess the authorities will be as anxious to catch those fellows as we are to have them," resumed Blake. "Putting a ship in danger of an attack from a submarine, as was undoubtedly done when Labenstein waved my flashlight, isn't a matter to be lightly passed over."

And the authorities took the same view. Soon after Captain Merceau had sent his report of the occurrence to London to the officials of the English war office, the boys were summoned before one of the officers directing the Secret Service and were closely questioned. They were asked to tell all they knew of the man calling himself Lieutenant Secor and the one who was on the passenger list as Levi Labenstein. This they did, relating everything from Charlie's accident with the Frenchman to the destruction of the submarine by the depth charge just after Labenstein had flashed his signal, assuming that this was what he had done.

"Very well, young gentlemen, I am exceedingly obliged to you," said the English officer. "The matter will be taken care of promptly and these men may be arrested. In that case, we shall want your evidence, so perhaps you had better let me know a little more about yourselves. I presume you have passports and the regulation papers?" and he smiled; but, as Blake said afterward, it was not exactly a trusting smile.

"He looked as if he'd like to catch us napping," Blake said.

However, the papers of the moving picture boys were in proper shape. But they were carefully examined, and during the process, when Joe, addressing Charles Anderson, spoke to him as "Macaroni," the officer looked up quickly.

"I thought his name was Charles," he remarked, as he referred to the papers.

"Certainly. But we call him 'Macaroni' sometimes because he looks like it - especially his legs," Joe explained.

"His legs macaroni?" questioned the English officer, regarding the three chums over the tops of his glasses. "Do you mean - er - that his legs are so easily broken - as macaroni is broken?"

"No, not that. It's because they're so thin," Joe added.

Still the officer did not seem to comprehend.

"It's a joke," added Blake.

Then the Englishman's face lit up.

"Oh, a joke!" he exclaimed. "Why didn't you say so at first? Now I comprehend. A joke! Oh, that's different! His legs are like macaroni, so you call him spaghetti! I see! Very good! Very good!" and he laughed in a ponderous way.

"At the same time," he went on, "I think I shall make a note of it. I will just jot it down on the margin of his papers, that he is called 'Macaroni' as a joke. Some other officer might not see the point," he added. "I'm quite fond of a joke myself! This is a very good one. I shall make a note of it." And this he proceeded to do in due form.

"Well, if that isn't the limit!" murmured Joe, when the officer, having returned their papers to them, sent them to another department to get the necessary passes by which they could claim their baggage and make application to go to the front.

"It's a good thing this officer had a sense of humor," remarked Blake, half sarcastically, "or we might have had to send back for a special passport for one stick of macaroni."

If Blake and his chums had an idea they would at once be permitted to depart for "somewhere in France" and begin the work of taking moving pictures of Uncle Sam's boys in training and in the trenches, they were very soon disillusioned. It was one thing to land in England during war times, but it was another matter to get out, especially when they were not English subjects.

It is true that Mr. Hadley had made arrangements for the films to be made, and they were to be taken for and under the auspices of the United States War Department.

But England has many institutions, and those connected with war are bound up in much red tape, in which they are not unlike our own, in some respects.

The applications of Blake and his chums to depart for the United States base in France were duly received and attached to the application already made by Mr.

Hadley and approved by the American commanding officer.

"And what happens next?" asked Blake, when they had filled out a number of forms in the English War Office. "I mean, where do we go from here?"

"Ah, that's one of your songs, isn't it?" asked an English officer, one who looked as though he could understand a joke better than could the one to whom macaroni so appealed.

"Yes, it's a song, but we don't want to stay here too long singing it," laughed Joe.

"Well, I'll do my best for you," promised the officer, who was a young man. He had been twice wounded at the front and was only awaiting a chance to go back, he said. "I'll do my best, but it will take a little time. We'll have to send the papers to France and wait for their return."

"And what are we to do in the meanwhile?" asked Blake.

"I fancy you'll just have to stay here and - what is it you say - split kindling?"

"'Saw wood,' I guess you mean," said Joe. "Well, if we have to, we have to. But please rush it along, will you?"

"I'll do my best," promised the young officer. "Meanwhile, you had better let me have your address - I mean the name of the hotel where you will be staying - and I'll send you word as soon as I get it myself. I had better tell you, though, that you will not be allowed to take any pictures - moving or other kind - until you have received permission."

"We'll obey that ruling," Blake promised. He had hoped to get some views of ruins caused by a Zeppelin. However, there was no hope of that.

On the recommendation of the young officer they took rooms in London at a hotel in a vicinity to enable them to visit the War Department easily. And then, having spent some time in these formalities and being again assured that they would be notified when they were wanted, either to be given permission to go to France or to testify against the two suspects, the moving picture boys went to their hotel.

It was not the first time they had been in a foreign country, though never before had they visited London, and they were much interested in everything they saw, especially everything which pertained to the war. And evidences of the war were on every side: injured and uninjured soldiers; poster appeals for enlistments, for the saving of food or money to win the war; and many other signs and mute testimonies of the great conflict.

The boys found their hotel a modest but satisfactory one, and soon got in the way of living there, planning to stay at least a week. They learned that their food would be limited in accordance with war regulations, but they had expected this.

There was something else, though, which they did not expect, and which at first struck them as being decidedly unpleasant. It was the second day of their stay in London that, as they were coming back to their hotel from a visit to a moving picture show, Joe remarked:

"Say, fellows, do you notice that man in a gray suit and a black slouch hat across the street?"

"I see him," admitted Blake.

"Have you seen him before?" Joe asked.

"Yes, I have," said Blake. "He was in the movies with us, and I saw him when we left the hotel."

"So did I," went on Joe. "And doesn't it strike you as being peculiar?"
"In what way?" asked Charles.

"I mean he seems to be following us."

"What in the world for?" asked the assistant.

"Well," went on Joe slowly, "I rather think we're under suspicion. That's the way it strikes me!"

CHAPTER XIV

IN CUSTODY

Blake and Charlie nodded their heads as Joe gave voice to his suspicion. Then, as they looked across once again at the man in the slouch hat, he seemed aware of their glances and slunk down an alley.

"But I think he has his eye on us, all the same," observed Blake, as the boys went into their hotel.

"What are we going to do about it?" inquired Charlie. "Shall we put up a kick or a fight?"

"Neither one," decided Blake, after a moment's thought.

"Why not?" inquired Macaroni, with rather a belligerent air, as befitted one in the midst of war's alarms. "Why not go and ask this fellow what he means by spying on us?"

"In the first place, if we could confront him, which I very much doubt," answered Blake, "he would probably deny that he was even so much as looking at us, except casually. Those fellows from Scotland Yard, or whatever the English now call their Secret Service, are as keen as they make 'em. We wouldn't get any satisfaction by kicking."

"Then let's fight!" suggested Charlie. "We can protest to the officer who told us to wait here for our permits to go to the front. We can say we're United States citizens and we object to being spied on. Let's do it!"

"Yes, we could do that," said Blake slowly. "But perhaps we are being kept under surveillance by the orders of that same officer."

"What in the world for?"

"Well, because the authorities may want to find out more about us."

"But didn't we have our passports all right? And weren't our papers in proper shape?" asked Charlie indignantly.

"As far as we ourselves are concerned, yes," said Blake. "But you must remember that passports have been forged before, by Germans, and -"

"I hope they don't take *us* for Germans!" burst out Charlie.

"Well, we don't look like 'em, that's a fact," said Blake, with a smile. "But you must remember that the English have been stung a number of times, and they aren't taking any more chances."

"Just what do you think this fellow's game is?" asked Charlie.

"Well," answered Blake slowly, and as if considering

all sides of the matter. "I think he has been detailed by the English Foreign Office, or Secret Service, or whoever has the matter in charge, to keep an eye on us and see if we are really what we claim to be. That's all. I don't see any particular harm in it; and if we objected, kicked, or made a row, it would look as if we might be guilty. So I say let it go and let that chap do all the spying he likes."

"Well, I guess you're right," assented Joe.

"Same here," came from their helper.

"Anyhow, we might as well make the best of it," resumed Blake. "If we had a fight with this chap and made him skedaddle, it would only mean another would be put on our trail. Just take it easy, and in due time, I think, we'll be given our papers and allowed to go to the front."

"It can't come any too soon for me," declared Joe.

So for the next few days the boys made it a point to take no notice of the very obvious fact that they were under surveillance. It was not always the same man who followed them or who was seen standing outside the hotel when they went out and returned. In fact, they were sure three different individuals had them in charge, so to speak.

The boys were used to active work with their cameras and liked to be in action, but they waited with as good grace as possible. In fact, there was nothing else to do. Their moving picture apparatus was sealed and kept in the Foreign Office, and would not be delivered to them until their permits came to go to the front. So, liking it or not, the boys had to submit.

They called several times on the young officer who had treated them so kindly, to ask whether there were any developments in their case; but each time they were told, regretfully enough, it seemed, that there was none.

"But other permits have been longer than yours in coming," said the officer, with a smile. "You must have a little patience. We are not quite as rapid as you Americans."

"But we want to get to the war front!" exclaimed Joe. "We want to make some pictures, and if we have to wait -"

"Possess your souls with patience," advised the officer. "The war is going to last a long, long time, longer than any of us have any idea of, I am afraid. You will see plenty of fighting, more's the pity. Don't fret about that."

But the boys did fret; and as the days passed they called at the permit office not once but twice, and, on one occasion, three times in twenty-four hours. The official was always courteous to them, but had the same answer:

"No news yet!"

And then, when they had spent two weeks in London - two weeks that were weary ones in spite of the many things to see and hear - the boys were rather surprised on the occasion of their daily visit to the permit office to be told by a subordinate:

"Just a moment, if you please. Captain Bedell wishes to speak to you."

The captain was the official who had their affair in charge, and who had been so courteous to them.

"He wants us to wait!" exclaimed Joe, with marked enthusiasm. For the last few days the captain had merely sent out word that there was no news.

"Maybe he has the papers!" cried Macaroni.

"I'm sure I hope so," murmured Blake.

The boys waited in the outer office with manifest impatience until the clerk came to summon them into the presence of Captain Bedell, saying:

"This way, if you please."

"Sounds almost like a dentist inviting you into his chair," murmured Joe to Blake.

"Not as bad as that, I hope. It looks encouraging to be told to wait and come in."

They were ushered into the presence of Captain Bedell, who greeted them, not with a smile, as he had always done before, but with a grave face.

Instantly each of the boys, as he admitted afterward, thought something was wrong.

"There's something out of the way with our passports," was Joe's idea.

"Been a big battle and the British have lost," guessed Macaroni.

Blake's surmise was:

"There's a hitch and we can't go to the front."

As it happened, all three were wrong, for a moment later, after he had asked them to be seated, Captain Bedell touched a bell on his desk. An orderly answered and he was told:

"These are the young gentlemen."

"Does that mean we are to get our permits?" asked Joe eagerly.

"I am sorry to say it does not," was the grave answer. "I am also sorry to inform you that you are in custody."

"In custody!" cried the three at once. And Blake a moment later added:

"On what grounds?"

"That I am not at liberty to tell you, exactly," the officer replied. "You are arrested under the Defense of the Realm Act, and the charges will be made known to you in due course of time."

"Arrested!" cried Joe. "Are we really arrested?"

"Not as civil but as military prisoners," went on Captain Bedell. "There is quite a difference, I assure you. I am sorry, but I have to do my duty. Orderly, take the prisoners away. You may send for counsel, of course," he added.

"We don't know a soul here, except some moving picture people to whom we have letters of introduction," Blake said despondently.

"Well, communicate with some of them," advised the captain. "They will be able to recommend a solicitor. Not that it will do you much good, for you will have to remain in custody for some time, anyhow."

"Are we suspected of being spies?" asked Joe, determined to hazard that question.

Captain Bedell smiled for the first time since the boys had entered his office. It was a rather grim contortion of the face, but it could be construed into a smile.

"I am not at liberty to tell you," he said. "Orderly, take the prisoners away, and give them the best of care, commensurate, of course, with safe-keeping."

CHAPTER XV

THE FRONT AT LAST

Well, wouldn't this get your -"

"Billiard table!" finished Joe for his chum Blake, who seemed at a loss for a word.

"Why billiard table?" asked Blake.

"Because they've sort of put the English on us!" And Joe laughed at his joke - if it could be called that.

"Huh!" grunted Blake, "I'm glad you feel so about it. But this is fierce! That's what I call it - fierce!"

"Worse than that!" murmured Charlie. "And the worst of it is they won't give us a hint what it's all about."

"There *is* a good deal of mystery about it," chimed in Joe.

"All but about the fact that we're in a jail, or the next thing to it," added Blake, with a look about the place where he and his chums had been taken from the office of Captain Bedell.

They were actually in custody, and while there were no

bars to the doors of their prison, which were of plain, but heavy, English oak, there were bars to the windows. Aside from that, they might be in some rather ordinary hotel suite, for there were three connecting rooms and what passed for a bath, though this seemed to have been added after the place was built.

As a matter of fact, the three boys were held virtually as captives, in a part of the building given over to the secret service work of the war. They had been escorted to the place by the orderly, who had instructions to treat his prisoners with consideration, and he had done that.

"This is one of our - er - best - apartments," he said, with an air of hesitation, as though he had been about to call it a cell but had thought better of it. "I hope you will be comfortable here."

"We might be if we knew what was going to happen to us and what it's all about," returned Blake, with a grim smile.

"That is information I could not give you, were I at liberty to do so, sir," answered the orderly. "Your solicitor will act for you, I have no doubt."

Following the advice of Captain Bedell, the boys had communicated with some of their moving picture friends in London, with the result that a solicitor, or lawyer, as he would be called in the United States, promised to act for the boys. He was soon to call to see them, and, mean-while, they were waiting in their "apartment."

"I wonder how it all happened?" mused Joe, as he looked from one of the barred windows at the not very cheerful prospect of roofs and chimneys.

"And what is the charge?" asked Charlie. "We can't even find that out."

"It practically amounts to being charged with being spies," said Blake. "That is what I gather from the way we are being treated. We are held as spies!"

"And Uncle Sam is fighting for the Allies!" cried Joe.

"Oh, well, it's all a mistake, of course, and we can explain it as soon as we get a chance and have the United States consul give us a certificate of good character," went on Blake. "That's what we've got to have our lawyer do when he comes - talk with the United States consul."

"Well, I wish he'd hurry and come," remarked Joe. "It is no fun being detained here. I want to get to the front and see some action. Our cameras will get rusty if we don't use them."

"That's right," agreed Macaroni.

It was not until the next day, however, that a solicitor came, explaining that he had been delayed after getting the message from the boys. The lawyer, as Blake and his friends called him, proved to be a genial gentleman who sympathized with the boys.

He had been in New York, knew something about moving pictures, and, best of all, understood the desire of the American youths to be free and to get into action.

"The first thing to be done," said Mr. Dorp, the solicitor, "is to find out the nature of the charge against you, and who made it. Then we will be in a position to act. I'll see Captain Bedell at once."

This he did, with the result that the boys were taken before the officer, who smiled at them, said he was sorry for what had happened, but that he had no choice in the matter.

"As for the nature of the charge against you, it is this," he said. "It was reported to us that you came here to get pictures of British defenses to be sold to Germany, and that your desire to go to the front, to get views of and for the American army, was only a subterfuge to cover your real purpose."

"Who made that charge?" asked Blake.

"It came in a letter to the War Department," was the answer, "and from some one who signed himself Henry Littlefield of New York City. He is in London, and he would appear when wanted, he said."

"May I see that letter?" asked the lawyer, and when it was shown to him he passed it over to the boys, asking if they knew the writer or recognized the handwriting.

And at this point the case of the prosecution, so to speak, fell through. For Blake, with a cry of surprise, drew forth from his pocket another letter, saying:

"Compare the writing of that with the letter denouncing us! Are they not both in the same hand?"

"They seem to be," admitted Captain Bedell, after an inspection.

"From whom is your letter?" asked Mr. Dorp.

"From Levi Labenstein, the man who summoned the submarine to sink the *Jeanne*," answered Blake. "This letter dropped from his pocket when he came to me to borrow the flashlight. I intended to give it back to him, as it is one he wrote to some friend and evidently forgot to mail. It contains nothing of importance, as far as I can see, though it may be in cipher. But this letter, signed with his name, is in the same hand as the one signed 'Henry Littlefield,' denouncing us."

"Then you think it all a plot?" asked Captain Bedell.

"Of course!" cried Joe. "Why didn't you say before, Blake, that you had a letter from this fellow?"

"I didn't attach any importance to it until I saw the letter accusing us. Now the whole thing is clear. He wants us detained here for some reason, and took this means of bringing it about."

"If that is the case, you will soon be cleared," said Captain Bedell.

And the boys soon were. There was no doubt but that the two letters were in the same hand. And when it was explained what part the suspected German had played aboard the steamer and cables from America to the United States consul had vouched for the boys, they were set free with apologies.

And what pleased them still more was Captain

Bedell's announcement:

"I also have the pleasure to inform you that the permits allowing you to go to the front have been received. They came yesterday, but, of course, under the circumstances I could not tell you."

"Then may we get on the firing line?" asked Blake.

"As soon as you please. We will do all we can to speed you on your way. It is all we can do to repay for the trouble you have had."

"These are war times, and one can't be too particular," responded Joe. "We don't mind, now that we can get a real start."

"I'd like to get at that fake Jew and the Frenchman who spoiled the films!" murmured Charles.

"Charlie can forgive everything but those spoiled films," remarked Blake, with a chuckle.

"We will try to apprehend the two men," promised Captain Bedell, "but I am afraid it is too late. It may seem strange to you that we held you on the mere evidence of a letter from a man we did not know. But you must remember that the nerves of every one are more or less upset over what has happened. The poison of Germany's spy system had permeated all of us, and nothing is normal. A man often suspects his best friend, so though it may have seemed unusual to you to be arrested, or detained, as we call it, still when all is considered it was not so strange.

"However, you are at liberty to go now, and we will do

all we can to help you. I have instructions to set you on your way to the front as soon as you care to go, and every facility will be given you to take all the pictures of your own troops you wish. I regret exceedingly what has happened."

"Oh, let it go!" said Blake cheerfully. "You treated us decently, and, as you say, these are war times."

"Which is my only excuse," said the captain, with a smile. "Now I am going to see if we can not apprehend that German and his French fellow-conspirator."

But, as may be guessed, "Henry Littlefield" was not to be found, nor Lieutenant Secor, nor Levi Labenstein.

"Labenstein probably wrote that letter accusing us and mailed it just to make trouble because we suspected him and Secor," said Blake.

"Well, it's lucky you had that note from him, or you'd never have been able to convince the authorities here that he was a faker," remarked Joe. "I guess he didn't count on that."

"Probably not," agreed Blake. "And now, boys, let's get busy!"

There was much to do after their release. They went back to their hotel and began getting their baggage in shape for the trip to France. Their cameras and reels were released from the custody of the war officials, and with a glad smile Macaroni began overhauling them to see that they had not been damaged on the trip.

"Right as ever!" he remarked, after a test. "Now they

can begin the *parlez vous Francaise?* business as soon as they please."

Two days later the boys embarked for the passage across the Channel, and though it was a desperately rough one, they were, by this time, seasoned travelers and did not mind it.

The journey through France up to the front was anything but pleasant. The train was slow and the cars uncomfor-table, but the boys made the best of it, and finally one afternoon, as the queer little engine and cars rolled slowly up to what served for a station, there came to their ears dull boomings.

"Thunder?" asked Joe, for the day was hot and sultry.

"Guns at the front," remarked a French officer, who had been detailed to be their guide the last part of the journey.

"At the front at last! Hurrah!" cried Joe.

"Perhaps you will not feel like cheering when you have been here a week or two," said the French officer.

"Sure we will!" declared Charlie. "We can do something now besides look at London chimney pots. We can get action!"

As the boys looked about on the beautiful little French village where they were to be quartered for some time, it was hard to realize that, a few miles away, men were engaged in deadly strife, that guns were booming, killing and maiming, and that soon they might be looking on the tangled barbed-wire defense of No

Man's Land.

But the dull booming, now and then rising to a higher note, told them the grim truth.

They were at the war front at last!

CHAPTER XVI

THE FIRING LINE

"Hello! Where are you fellows from?"

It was rather a sharp challenge, yet not unfriendly, that greeted Blake, Joe and Charlie, as they were walking from the house where they had been billeted, through the quaint street of the still more quaint French village. "Where are you from?"

"New York," answered Blake, as he turned to observe a tall, good-natured-looking United States infantryman regarding him and his two chums.

"New York, eh? I thought so! I'm from that burg myself, when I'm at home. Shake, boys! You're a sight for sore eyes. Not that I've got 'em, but some of the fellows have - and worse. From New York! That's mighty good! Shake again!"

And they did shake hands all around once more.

"My name's Drew - Sam Drew," announced the private. "I'm one of the doughboys that came over first with Pershing. Are you newspaper fellows?"

"No. Moving picture," answered Blake.

"You don't say so! That's great! Shake again. When are you going to give a show?"

"Oh, we're not that kind," explained Joe. "We're here to take army films."

"Oh, shucks!" cried Private Drew. "I thought we were to see something new. The boys here are just aching for something new. There's a picture show here, but the machine's busted and nobody can fix it. We had a few reels run off, but that's all. Say, we're 'most dead from what these French fellows call *ong we*, though o-n-g-w-e ain't the way you spell it. If we could go to one show -"

"You say there's a projector here?" interrupted Joe eagerly.

"Well, I don't know what you call it, but there's a machine here that showed some pictures until it went on the blink."

"Maybe I can fix it," went on Joe, still eagerly. "Let's have a look at it. But where do you get current from? This town hasn't electric lights."

"No, but we've got a gasolene engine and a dynamo. The officers' quarters and some of the practice trenches are lighted by electricity. Oh, we have some parts of civilization here, even if we are near the trenches!"

"If you've got current and that projection machine isn't too badly broken, maybe I can fix her up," said Joe. "Let's have a look at it."

"Oh, I'll lead you to it, all right, Buddy!" cried Private

Drew. "We'll just eat up some pictures if we can get 'em! Come along! This way for the main show!" and he laughed like a boy.

Among the outfits sent with the troops quartered in this particular sector was a moving picture machine and many reels of film. But, as Sam Drew had said, the machine was broken.

After Blake and his chums had reported to the officer to whom they had letters of introduction and had been formally given their official designation as takers of army war films, they went to the old barn which had been turned into a moving picture theater.

There was a white cloth screen and a little gallery, made in what had been the hay mow, for the projector machine. Joe Duncan, as the expert mechanician of the trio, at once examined this, and said it could soon be put in readiness for service.

"Whoop!" yelled Private Drew, who seemed to have constituted himself the particular guide and friend of the moving picture boys. "Whoop! that's as good as getting a letter from home! Go to it, Buddy!"

And that first night of the boys' stay at that particular part of France was the occasion of a moving picture show. All who could crowded into the barn, and the reels were run over and over again as different relays of officers and men attended. For the officers were as eager as the privates, and the moving picture boys were welcomed with open arms.

"You sure did make a hit!" laughed Private Drew. "Yes, a sure-fire hit! Now let Fritz bang away. We should worry!"

But all was not moving pictures for Blake, Joe and their assistant, nor for the soldier boys, either. There was hard and grim work to do in order to be prepared for the harder and grimmer work to come. The United States troops were going through a period of intensive trench training to be ready to take their share of the fighting with the French and British forces.

The village where Blake and his chums were quartered was a few miles from the front, but so few that day and night, save when there was a lull, the booming of guns could be heard.

"There hasn't been much real fighting, of late," Private Drew informed the boys the day after their arrival. "It's mostly artillery stuff, and our boys are in that. Now and then a party of us goes over the top or on night listening-patrol. Fritz does the same, but, as yet, we haven't had what you could call a good fight. And we're just aching for it, too."

"That's what we want to get pictures of," said Blake. "Real fighting at the front trenches!"

"Oh, you'll get it," prophesied the private. "There's a rumor that we'll have some hot stuff soon. Some of our aircraft that have been strafing Fritz report that there's something doing back of the lines. Shouldn't wonder but they'll try to rush us some morning. That is, if we don't go over the top at 'em first."

"I hope we'll be there!" murmured Joe. "And I hope we get a good light so we can film the fighting."

"They'll be almost light enough from the star-shells, bombs and big guns," said Private Drew. "Say, you ought to see the illumination some nights when the Boches start to get busy! Coney Island is nothing to it, Buddy!"

Before the moving picture boys could get into real action on the front line trenches, there were certain formalities to
go through, and they had to undergo a bit of training.

Captain Black, to whom they were responsible and to whom they had to report each day, wanted first some films of life in the small village where the troops were quartered when not in the trenches. This was to show the "boys at home" what sort of life was in prospect for them.

Aside from the danger ever present in war in any form, life in the quaint little town was pleasant. The boys in khaki were comfortably housed, they had the best of army food, and their pleasures were not few. With the advent of Blake and his chums and the putting in operation of the moving picture show, enthusiasm ran high, and nothing was too good for the new arrivals.

But they had their work to do, for they were official photographers and were entrusted with certain duties. Back of the firing line, of course, there was no danger, unless from air raids. But after the first week, during which they took a number of reels of drilling and recreation scenes, there came a period of preparation.

Blake, Joe and Charlie were given gas masks and shown how to use them. They were also each provided with an automatic pistol and were given uniforms. For they had to be on the firing line and on such occasions were not really of the non-combatant class, though they were not supposed to take part in the fighting unless it should be to protect themselves.

At the suggestion of Captain Black the boys had made sheet-iron cases for their cameras and reels of film.

"Of course, if a shell comes your way that case won't be much protection," said the United States officer. "But shrapnel won't go through it."

Steel helmets were also given the boys to wear when they went on duty in the firing trenches, and they were told under no circumstances to leave them off.

"For even if there isn't any shooting from across No Man's Land," explained Captain Black, "a hostile aircraft may drop a bomb that will scatter a lot of steel bullets around. So wear your helmets and keep the cases on your cameras."

It was a week after this, during which time there had been several false alarms of a big German attack, that one evening as they were about to turn in after having given a moving picture show an orderly came up to Blake.

"You and your two friends will report to Captain Black at four o'clock to-morrow morning," said the orderly.

"Why that hour?" asked Joe curiously.

"We're going over the top," was the answer. "You may get some pictures then."

Charles Anderson hastily consulted a small book he took from his pocket.

"What you doing?" asked Blake.

"Looking to see what time the sun rises. I want to see if there'll be light enough to make pictures. Yes," he went on, as he found what he wanted in the miniature almanac, "we ought to be able to get some shots."

The gray wreaths of a fog that had settled down in the night were being dispelled by the advance heralds of dawn in the shape of a few faint streaks of light when Blake and his chums, wearing their steel helmets and with the steel-protected cameras, started from the farmhouse where they were quartered to report to Captain Black.

"All ready, boys?" the captain called. "We're going over the top at five-seven - just as soon as the artillery puts down a barrage to clear the way for us. You're to get what pictures you can. I'll leave that part to you. But don't get ahead of the barrage fire - that is, if you want to come back," he added significantly.

"All right," answered Blake, in a low voice.

He and his chums took their places in one of the communicating trenches, waiting for the American and the French soldiers in the front ones to spring up and go "over the top."

Every minute seemed an hour, and there were frequent consultations of wrist watches. Suddenly, at five o'clock exactly, there was a roar that sounded like a hundred bursts of thunder. The artillery had opened the engagement, and the moving picture boys, at last on the firing line, grasped their cameras and reels of film as the soldiers grasped their guns and waited for the word to go.

The earth beneath them seemed to rock with the concussion of the big guns.

CHAPTER XVII

BOWLED OVER

Not a man of the American and French forces that were to attack the Germans had yet left the protecting trench. The object of the artillery fire, which always preceded an attack unless it was a surprise one with tanks, was to blow away the barbed-wire entanglements, and, if possible, dispose of some of the enemy guns as well as the fighting men.

The barrage was really a "curtain of fire" moving ahead of the attacking troops to protect them. This curtain actually advanced, for the guns belching out the rain of steel and lead were slowly elevated, and with the elevation a longer range was obtained.

Waiting in a trench slightly behind the troops that were soon to go into action, Blake Stewart and his chums talked, taking no care to keep down their voices. Indeed, they had to yell to be heard.

"Well, we're here at last," said Blake.

"Yes; and it looks as if there'd be plenty of action," added Joe.

"If it only gets lighter and the smoke doesn't hang

down so," added Charlie. "We won't get very good films if it doesn't get lighter. It's fierce now."

"Well, if the fighting lasts long enough the sun will soon be higher and the light better," responded Blake. "And it sounds as if this was going to be a big fight."

By this time the German guns seemed to have awakened, and were replying to the fire from the American and French artillery. The shells flew screaming over the heads of those in the trenches, and instinctively Blake and his companions ducked.

Then they realized how futile this was. As a matter of fact, the shells were passing high over them and exploding even back of the line of cannon. For the Germans did not yet have the range, some of the Allies' guns having been moved up during the night.

Suddenly, though how the signal was given the moving picture boys did not learn until afterward, there was activity in the trenches before them. With yells that sounded only faintly above the roar of the big guns, the American and French soldiers went "over the top," and rushed toward the German trenches.

"Come on!" cried Blake. "This is our chance!"

"It isn't light enough!" complained Charlie, as he ran along the communicating trench with the other two lads to the front line ditch. "We can't get good pictures now."

"It's getting lighter!" cried Blake. "Come on!"

He and Joe were to work the cameras, with Charles

Anderson to stand by with spare reels of film, and to lend a helping hand if need be.

Along the narrow trench they rushed, carrying their machines which, it was hoped, would catch on the sensitive celluloid the scenes, or some of them, that were taking place in front. Mad scenes they were, too - scenes of bursting shells, of geysers of rock and earth being tossed high by some explosion, of men rushing forward to take part in the deadly combat.

As Blake had said, the scene was lighting up now. The sun rose above the mists and above the smoke of the guns, for though some smokeless powder was used, there was enough of the other variety to produce great clouds of vapor.

Behind the line of rushing soldiers, who were all firing their rifles rapidly, rushed the moving picture boys. They were looking for a spot on which to set their machines to get good views of the engagement.

"This'll do!" yelled Blake, as they came to a little hill, caused by the upheaval of dirt in some previous shell explosion. "We can stand here!"

"All right!" agreed Joe. "I'll go a little to one side so we won't duplicate."

The barrage fire had lifted, biting deeper into the ranks and trenches of the Germans. But they, on their part, had found the range more accurately, and were pouring an answering bombardment into the artillery stations of the French and Americans.

And then, as the sun came out clear, the boys had a

wonderful view of what was going on. Before them the French and Uncle Sam's boys were fighting with the Germans, who had been driven from their trenches. On all sides were rifles belching fire and sending out the leaden messengers of death.

And there, in the midst of the fighting but off to one side and out of the line of direct fire, stood Blake, Joe and Charlie, the two former turning the handles of the cameras and taking pictures even as they had stood in the midst of the volcanoes and earthquakes, or in the perils of the deep, making views.

The fighting became a mad riot of sound - the sound of big guns and little - the sound of bursting shells from either side - the yells of the men - the shouting of the officers and the shrill cries of the wounded.

It took all the nerve of the three lads to stand at their posts and see men killed and maimed before their eyes, but they were under orders, and did not waver. For these scenes, terrible and horrible though they were, were to serve the good purpose of stimulating those at home, in safety across the sea, to a realization of the perils of war and the menace of the Huns.

The fighting was now at its fiercest. The Germans had an accurate idea of the location of the American and French cannon by this time, and the artillery duel was taking place, while between that double line of fire the infantry were at body-grips.

Hand grenades were being tossed to and fro. Men were emptying the magazines of their rifles or small arms fairly into the faces of each other.

When a soldier's ammunition gave out, or his gun choked from the hot fire, he swung the rifle as a club or used the bayonet. And then came dreadful scenes - scenes that the moving picture boys did not like to think about afterward. But war is a grim and terrible affair, and they were in the very thick of it.

Suddenly, as Blake and Joe were grinding away at their cameras, now and then shifting them to get a different view, something that made shrill whistling sounds, passed over their heads.

"What's that?" asked Charlie, who stood ready with a reel of spare film for Blake's machine.

"Bullets, I reckon," answered Joe. "They seem to be coming our way, too."

"Maybe we'd better get out of here," suggested Blake. "We've got a lot of views, and -"

"Don't run yet, Buddies!" called a voice, and along came Private Drew. "You'll never hear the bullet that hits you. And they're firing high, the Fritzes are! Don't run yet. How're you making it?"

"All right so far, but it's - fierce!" cried Blake, as he stopped for a moment to let a smoke cloud blow away.

"Yes, it's a hot little party, all right," replied the soldier, with a grin. "I haven't had all my share yet. Had to go back with an order. Hi, here comes one!" and instinctively he dodged, as did the others, though a moment later it was borne to them that it was of little use to dodge on the battlefield.

Something flew screaming and whining over their heads, and fell a short distance away.

"It's a shell!" cried Joe, as he saw it half bury itself in the earth. "Look out!"

Private Drew gave one look at the place where the German missile had fallen, not ten feet away, and then, with a shrug of his shoulders, he cried:

"It's only a dud!"

"What's that?" asked Joe.

"Shell that didn't explode," answered the soldier. "The Fritzes have fired a lot of them lately. Guess their ammunition must be going back on them. It's only a dud!"

He was about to pass on, and the moving picture boys were going to resume their making of films, when another scream and whine like the first came, but seemingly nearer.

Instinctively all four looked up, and saw something flashing over their heads. They could feel the wind of the shell, for that is what it was, and then the chance shot from the German gun fell about fifty feet behind the group.

The next instant there was a tremendous explosion, and Blake and the others felt themselves being tossed about and knocked down as by a mighty wind.

CHAPTER XVIII

TRENCH LIFE

Blake was the first to scramble to his feet, rolling out from beneath a pile of dirt and stones that had been tossed on him as the shell heaved up a miniature geyser and covered him with the debris. Then, after a shake, such as a dog gives himself when he emerges from the water, and finding himself, as far as he could tell, uninjured, he looked to his companions.

Private Drew was staggering about, holding his right hand to his head, and on his face was a look of grim pain. But it passed in an instant as he cried to Blake:

"Hurt Buddy?"

"I don't seem to be," was the answer, given during a lull in the bombardment and firing. "But I'm afraid -"

He did not finish the sentence, but looked apprehensively at his prostrate chums. Both Joe and Charlie lay motion-less, half covered with dirt. One camera had been upset and the tripod was broken. The other, which Blake had been operating, seemed intact.

"Maybe they're only knocked out. That happens lots of times," said Drew. "We'll have a look."

"But you're hurt yourself!" exclaimed Blake, looking at a bloody hand the soldier removed from his head.

"Only a scratch, Buddy! A piece of the shell grazed me. First I thought it had taken me for fair, but it's only a scratch. If I don't get any worse than that I'm lucky. Now to have a look at your bunkies."

Charles Anderson seemed to need little looking after, for he arose to his feet, appearing somewhat dazed, but not hurt, as far as was evidenced.

"What happened?" he asked.

"Just a little bit of a compliment from our friend Fritz," answered Drew. "That was a real shell - no dud - but it exploded far enough away from us not to do an awful lot of damage. That is, unless your other bunkie is worse hurt."

"I'm afraid he is," observed Blake, for Joe had not yet moved, and dirt covered him thickly.

The center of the fighting seemed to have passed beyond the group of moving picture boys by this time. Blake, Charlie and Drew turned to where Joe lay and began scraping the dirt from him.

He stirred uneasily while they were doing this, and murmured:

"It's all right. Put in another reel."

"Touched on the head," said the soldier. "We'd better get him back of the lines where he can see a doctor. Your machine got a touch of it, too."

Anderson hurried over to the overturned camera. A quick examination showed him that it had suffered no more damage than the broken support.

"It's all right," he announced. "Not even light-struck, I guess. I'll take this and the boxes of film," and he shouldered his burden.

"Well, I'll take your bunkie - guess I can manage to carry him better than you, for we've had practice in that - and you can shoulder the other picture machine," said Drew, as he moved over to Joe. "We won't wait for the stretcher-men. They won't be along for some time if this keeps up. Come on now."

"But can you manage, hurt as you are?" asked Blake.

"Oh, sure! Mine's only a scratch. Wait, I'll give myself a little first aid and then I'll be all right."

With the help of Blake the soldier disinfected his wound with a liquid he took from his field kit, and then, having bound a bandage around his head, he picked up the still unconscious Joe and started back with him to the rear trenches.

They had to make a detour to avoid some of the German fire, which was still hot in sections, but finally managed to get to a place of comparative safety. Here they were met by a party of ambulance men, and Joe was placed on a stretcher and taken to a first dressing station.

Meanwhile, Anderson put the cameras with their valuable reels of film in a bomb-proof structure.

"Is he badly hurt?" asked Blake anxiously of the surgeon.

"I hope not. In fact, I think not," was the reassuring answer of the American army surgeon. "He has been shocked, and there is a bad bruise on one side, where he seems to have been struck by a stone thrown by the exploding shell. But a few days' rest will bring him around all right. Pretty close call, was it?"

"Oh, it might have been worse," answered Drew, whose wound had also been attended to. "It was just a chance shot."

"Well, I don't know that it makes an awful lot of difference whether it's a chance shot or one that is aimed at you, as long as it hits," said the surgeon. "However, you are luckily out of it. How does it seem, to be under fire?" he asked Blake.

"Well, I can't say I fancy it as a steady diet, and yet it wasn't quite as bad as I expected. And we got the pictures all right."

"That's good!" the surgeon said. "Well, your friend will be all right. He's coming around nicely now," for Joe was coming out of the stupor caused by the blow on the head from a clod of earth.

At first he was a bit confused - "groggy," Private Drew called it - but he soon came around, and though he could not walk because of the injury to his side, he was soon made comparatively comfortable and taken to a hospital just behind the lines.

As this was near the house where Charlie and Blake

were quartered, they could easily visit their chum each day, which they did for the week that he was kept in bed.

As Charles had surmised, the films in the cameras were not damaged, and were removed to be sent back for development. The broken tripod was repaired sufficiently to be usable again, and then the boys began to prepare for their next experience.

The engagement in which Joe had been hurt was a comparatively small one, but it netted a slight advance for the French and American troops, and enabled a little straightening of their trench line to be made, a number of German dug-outs having been demolished and their machine guns captured. This, for a time at least, removed a serious annoyance to those who had to occupy the front line trenches.

Though Joe improved rapidly in the hospital, for some time his side was very sore. He had to turn his camera over to Charlie, and it was fortunate the lanky helper had been brought along, for the work would have proved too much for Blake alone.

Following that memorable, because it was the first, going "over the top," there was a period of comparative quiet. Of course there was sniping day and night, and not a few casualties from this form of warfare, but it was to be expected and "all in the day's work," as Private Drew called it.

Blake, Joe and Charlie were complimented by Captain Black for their bravery in going so close to the front line in getting the pictures; then he added:

"You can have it a little easier for a while. What we want now are some scenes of trench life as it exists before an engagement. So get ready for that."

This Blake and Charlie did, while Joe sat in the sun and tried to learn French from a little boy, the son of the couple in whose house the moving picture boys were quartered.

Though the American and French soldiers, with here and there a Canadian or English regiment, lived so near the deadly front line, there were periods, some lengthy, of quiet and even amusement. Of course, the deaths lay heavy on all the soldiers when they allowed themselves to think of their comrades who had perished. And more than one gazed with wet eyes at the simple wooden crosses marking the graves "somewhere in France."

But officers and men alike knew how fatal to spirit it was to dwell on the sad side of war. So, as much as possible, there was in evidence a sense of lightness and a feeling that all was for the best - that it must be for the best.

Now and then there were night raids, and occasionally parties of German prisoners were brought in. Blake and Charlie made moving pictures of these as they were taken back to the cages. Most of the Germans seemed glad to be captured, which meant that they were now definitely out of the terrible scenes of the war. They would be held in safety until after the conflict, and they seemed to know this, for they laughed and joked as they were filmed. They appeared to like it, and shouted various words of joking import in their guttural voices to the boys.

A week after coming out of the hospital Joe was able to take up light work, and did his share of making pictures of trench life. He had a big bruise on one side, a discolored patch that had an unpleasant look, but which soon ceased to give much pain except after a period of exertion.

"Well, you're a veteran now - been wounded," said Blake to his chum.

"Yes, I suppose you can call it that. I don't care for any more, though."

The plan in operation at this particular section of the front where the moving picture boys were quartered and on duty was for the soldiers to spend five or six days in the trenches, taking turns of duty near No Man's Land, and then going back to rest in the dug-outs. After that they would have a day or so of real rest back of the lines, out of reach of the big guns.

And there the real fun of soldiering, if fun it can be called amid the grim business of war, was to be had. The officers and men vied with one another in trying to forget the terrible scenes through which they had gone, and little entertainments were gotten up, the moving picture boys doing their share.

Thus they obtained views of trench life both grave and gay, though it must be admitted that the more serious predominated. There were many wounded, many killed, and, occasionally, one of the parties going out on patrol or listening-duty at night would never come back, or, at most, one or two wounded men would come in to tell of a terrific struggle with a party of Huns.

Sometimes, though, the tale would be the other way around, and the Americans would come in with a number of captives who showed the effects of severe fighting.

CHAPTER XIX

GASSED

"Well, there's one thing about it," remarked Joe to Blake one day, as they sat in the shade beside the French cottage waiting for orders. "This isn't as nervous work as traveling on a ship, waiting for a submarine."

It was three weeks after the first and only engagement they had taken part in, and, meanwhile, they had filmed many more peaceful scenes of army life on the front.

"Especially when you know there's a traitor in the cabin across the hall that may signal any minute for you to be blown up," Blake responded to his friend's remark. "You're right there, Joe. But how's the side?"

"Coming on all right. Hurts hardly at all now. I wonder what became of those two fellows?"

"Which two?"

"Secor and Labenstein."

"Oh, I thought you meant those two German officers who tried to hire us to send some word back to their folks about them."

This had been the case: In a batch of prisoners brought in after a raid which was most successful on the part of the Americans, two captured German officers of high rank who spoke English well had offered Blake and Joe a large sum if they would send word of their fate and where they were held prisoners to an address in Berlin.

But the boys would do nothing of the sort, and reported the matter to Captain Black. The result was that the officers were searched and some valuable papers, containing some future plans of the enemy, were discovered. The officers were sent to England under a strong guard, as it was felt they were particularly dangerous.

"I suppose Secor and Labenstein are somewhere, plotting to do their worst," went on Blake. "Having gone as far as they did, they wouldn't give up easily, I imagine. I can understand Labenstein's acting as he did, but that Secor, a Frenchman, if he really is one, should plot to injure his own country - that gets me!"

"Same here! I wonder if we'll ever see him again - either of them, for that matter."

"I hope not I don't like - snakes!" exclaimed Blake.

"Yes, that's what they are - snakes in the grass," agreed Joe. "But I wonder what our next assignment will be."

"It's hard to say. Here comes an orderly now. Maybe he has some instructions."

This proved to be the case, the messenger bearing a note from Captain Black, requesting the moving picture boys to get some scenes around the camp when the soldiers were served with their daily rations.

Some German propaganda was being circulated in the United States, Captain Black explained, to the effect that the soldiers in France were being underfed and were most unhappy. It was said that large losses had taken place in their ranks through starvation.

"We want to nail that lie to the mast!" said the captain; "and I can't imagine a better way than by making some films showing the boys at their meals."

"And they are some meals, too!" exclaimed Blake, as he and his chum made ready for the task set them. "If every soldier in this war had as good grub as our boys, they'd want to keep on fighting."

Though Blake and Joe were resting at that particular time, it must not be assumed that they did much of that sort of thing. Of course they were not always on duty. Moreover, unlike the soldiers, they could do nothing after dark, during which period many raids were made on both sides. The moving picture business of taking films depended on daylight for its success. But when they were not filming peaceful scenes in and about the trenches the boys were getting views of tanks, of men drilling, of their games and sports, and now they were to get some pictures of the meals.

As Blake and Joe had remarked, they had neither heard nor seen anything of Secor or Labenstein since they came from England. The men might have been arrested, but this was hardly likely.

"Even if they were we wouldn't hear of it," said Blake. "But I hope, if they are under arrest, they'll hold them until we can tell what we know of them."

"Same here," agreed Joe. "But I guess we'll never see them again."

Before long, however, his words were recalled to him in a strange manner and under grim circumstances.

"Well, Buddy, coming to get yours?" called Private Drew, as Blake and Joe, their cameras over their shoulders, walked toward the cook wagons from which came fragrant odors.

"Haven't heard any invitations yet," returned Blake, grinning.

"Come in with us!"

"Over this way!"

"Here you are for the big feed!"

The cries came from a number of different groups of Uncle Sam's soldiers who were fighting in France. For Blake, Joe and Charlie were generally liked, and though they were not supposed to mess with the soldiers, they did so frequently, and had many a good meal in consequence.

"We're going to get records of your appetites to show the folks back home," observed Blake, as he and Joe set up the machines. "There's a report that you're gradually wasting away from lack of pie and cake."

"Watch me waste!" cried a vigorous specimen of American manhood. "Just watch me waste!" And he held aloft a big plate heaped high with good and substantial food, while, laughing, Blake and Joe made ready to get the views.

There was much fun and merriment, even though a few miles away there was war in its grimmest aspect But if one thought of that all the while, as Captain Black said, none would have the nerve and mental poise to face the guns and finally overcome the Huns.

Following the taking of the scenes around the mess hall, others were made showing the boys in khaki at bayonet practice, at the throwing of hand grenades, and other forms of war exercises.

"I guess these will do for peaceful scenes," said Captain Black, when Joe and Blake reported to him what they had accomplished. "And now do you feel equal to a little more strenuous work?"

"Yes, sir. In what way?" returned Blake.

"On the firing line again. I know you'll keep it to yourselves, but we are going to have a big engagement in a day or so. We are all primed for it and it will be on a big scale. The Government wants some films of it, if you can get them, films not so much to be shown in public as to be official records of the War Department. Do you boys feel equal to the task?"

"That's what we're here for!" exclaimed Blake.

"How about you, Duncan?" asked the captain of Joe. "Is your side all right?"

"Oh, yes! I'd never know I'd been hurt. I'm game, all right!"

"Well, it will be in a day or so. None of us knows exactly when, as those higher up don't let us into all of their secrets. Too many leaks, you know. We want to surprise Fritz if we can."

This gave the moving picture boys something further to think about and to plan for, and when they had taken the reels of exposed film, showing the dinner scenes, from their cameras, they made the machines ready for more strenuous work.

"I think I'll put an extra covering of thin sheet steel on the film boxes," said Charlie, talking the matter over with his two chums. "A stray bit of shrapnel might go through them now and make a whole reel light-struck."

"I suppose it would be a good idea," agreed Blake. "Go to it, Mac, and we'll be ready when you are."

Four days of anxious waiting followed, with the men keyed up to concert pitch, so to speak, and eager for the word to come that would send them out of the trenches and against the ranks of the Germans.

But for a long time no word came from the higher command to prepare for the assault, though many knew it was pending. Perhaps the Germans knew it, too, and that was what caused the delay. None could say.

Blake, Joe and Charlie were in readiness. They had their cameras adjusted, had plenty of fresh film, and but awaited the word that would send them from their comparatively comfortable house with the French family into the deadly trenches.

Finally the word came. Once more in the gray dawn the boys took their places with their cameras in the communicating trench, while ahead of them crouched the soldiers eager to be unleashed at the Germans.

And then they went through it all over again. There was the curtain of fire, the artillery opening up along a five-mile front with a din the boys had never heard equalled.

Waiting for the light to improve a little, the boys set up their cameras in a little grove of trees where they would be somewhat protected and began to make the pictures.

The battle was one of the worst of the war. There were many killed and wounded, and through it all - through the storm of firing - the moving picture boys took reel after reel of film.

"Some fight!" cried Blake, as a screaming shell burst over their heads, some scattering fragments falling uncomfortably close to them.

"I should say yes!" agreed Joe. "But look, here comes Drew on the run. I wonder what's happened."

They saw their friend the private rushing toward them, and waving his hands. He was shouting, but what he said they could not hear.

And then, so suddenly that it was like a burst of fire, Blake, Joe and Charles experienced a strange feeling!

Some powerful odor overpowered them! Gasping and choking, they fell to the ground, dimly hearing Drew shouting:

"Gassed! Gassed! Put on your masks!"

CHAPTER XX

"GONE!"

Rolling down upon the American and French battle-lines, coming out of the German trenches, where it had been generated as soon as it was noted that the wind was right, drifted a cloud of greenish yellow, choking chlorine gas.

Chlorine gas is made by the action of sulphuric acid and manganese dioxide on common salt. It has a peculiar corrosive effect on the nose, throat and lungs, and is most deadly in its effect. It is a heavy gas, and instead of rising, as does hydrogen, one of the lightest of gases, it falls to the ground, thus making it dangerously effective for the Huns. They can depend on the wind to blow it to the enemy's trenches and fill them as would a stream of water.

Knowing as he did the deadly nature of the gas from his own experience and that of his comrades, some of whom had been killed by it, Private Drew lost no time in sounding his warning to the moving picture boys. He had taken part in the raid on the Germans, had seen and engaged in some hard fighting, and had been sent to the rear with an order from his officer. And it was as he started that he saw, from one section of the Hun lines, the deadly gas rolling out.

He knew from the direction and strength of the wind just where it would reach to, and, seeing the moving picture boys in its path, he called to them.

"Put on your masks! Put on your masks!" cried the soldier. At the same time, as he ran, he loosed his from where it hung at his belt and began to don it.

The gas masks used in the trenches are simple affairs. They consist of a cloth helmet which is saturated with a chemical that neutralizes the action of the chlorine. There are two celluloid eye holes and a rubber tube, which is taken into the mouth and through which the air breathed is expelled. All air breathed, mixed as it is with the deadly chlorine, passes through the chemical-saturated cloth of the helmet and is thus rendered harmless. But it is a great strain on those who wear the masks, for nothing like the right kind of breathing can be done. In fact, a diver at the bottom of the sea has better and more pure air to breathe than a soldier in the open wearing a gas mask.

It was the first experience of Blake and his chums with the German gas, though they had heard much about it, and it needed but the first whiff to make them realize their danger.

Even as Private Drew called to them, and as they saw him running toward them and trying to adjust his own mask, they were overcome. As though shot, they fell to the ground, their eyes smarting and burning, their throats and nostrils seeming to be pinched in giant fingers, and their hearts laboring.

One moment they had been operating their cameras. The next they were bowled over.

"Put on your -" began Blake; and then he could say no more. He tried not to breathe as he fumbled at his belt to loosen his mask. He buried his nose deep in the cool earth, but such is the nature of this gas that it seeks the lowest level. There is no getting away from it save by going up.

In a smoke-filled room a fireman may find a stratum of cool, and comparatively fresh, air at the bottom near the floor. This is because cold air is heavier than the hot and smoke-filled atmosphere. But this does not hold with the German gas.

And so, before Blake could slip over his head the chemical-impregnated cloth, he lost consciousness. In another moment his two companions were also unconscious. Private Drew, struggling against the terrible pressure on his lungs, managed to get his helmet over his head, and then he gave his attention to his friends.

He knew that to save their lives he must get their helmets on; for a few breaths of the gas will not kill. But they will disable a person for some time, and a little longer breathing of it means a horrible death.

And so, working at top speed, the soldier, now himself protected from the fumes, though he had breathed more of them than he liked, labored to save his friends.

Suddenly a new terror developed, for, wearing their own helmets which made them look like horrible monsters out of a nightmare, the Germans charged against the French and Americans, whom they hoped to find disabled by the gas.

"Here they come with blood in their eyes if I could only see it!" mused Private Drew, as he finished fastening the helmet on Charles Anderson, having already thus protected Joe and Blake. All three boys were now unconscious, and what the outcome would be the soldier could only guess.

"But there won't be any guesswork if I leave 'em here for the Huns," he reasoned. "I've got to help 'em back - but how?"

The Germans, in a counter-offensive, were striving to regain some of the lost ground, and, for the moment, were driving before them the French and American forces. Back rushed the advance lines to their supporting columns, and Drew, seeing some of his own messmates, signaled to them, for he could not talk with the helmet on.

Fortunately his chums of the trenches understood, and while some of them caught up the unconscious boys and started with them to the rear, others saved the moving picture machines.

And then, just as it seemed that the Germans would overtake them and dispose of the whole party, there came a rush of helmet-protected Americans who speedily dispersed those making the counter-attack, pursuing them back to the very trenches which they had left not long before.

The fight went on in that gas-infested territory, a grim fight, desperate and bloody, but in which the Allies were at last successful, though Blake and his two chums saw nothing of it.

"They're in a bad way," the surgeon said, when he examined them soon after Drew and his friends brought them in. "I don't know whether we can save them."

But prompt action, coupled with American ingenuity and the knowledge that had been gained from the experience of French and British surgeons in treating cases of gas poisoning, eventually brought the moving picture boys back to the life they had so nearly left.

It was several days, though, before they were out of danger, and by that time the French and Americans had consolidated the gains it cost them so much to make, so that the place where the three boys had been overcome was now well within the Allied lines.

"Well, what happened to us?" asked Joe, when he and his chums were able to leave the hospital.

"You were gassed," explained Private Drew, who had had a slight attack himself. "Didn't you hear me yelling at you to put on your helmets?"

"Yes, and we started to do it," said Blake. "But that stuff works like lightning."

"Glad you found that out, anyhow," grimly observed the soldier. "The next time you hear the warning, 'Gas!' don't stop to think, just grab your helmet. And don't wait longer than to feel a funny tickling in your nose, as if you wanted to sneeze but couldn't. Most likely that'll be gas, too. Cover your head when you feel that."

"Thanks!" murmured Blake, for he and his chums

understood that the soldier and his mates had saved their lives.

Now that the moving picture boys were out of danger and could take some stock of themselves and their surroundings, their first thoughts, naturally, were of their apparatus.

"Did they get our machines?" asked Joe.

"No; we saved the cameras for you," answered Drew.

"What about the boxes of exposed film - the ones the War Office is so anxious to get?" asked Blake.

"I didn't see anything of them," said the soldier. "We were too anxious to get you out of the gas and save the cameras to think of anything else. I didn't see any boxes of films, but I'll ask some of the boys who helped me."

Blake and his chums waited for this information anxiously, and when it came it was a disappointment, for no one knew anything of the valuable reels.

"Though they may be there yet," said Drew. "There was some fierce fighting around that shell crater where we carried you from, but it's within our lines now, and maybe the boxes are there yet. Better go and take a look."

This Blake, Joe and Charlie lost no time in doing. After a little search, for the character of the ground had so changed by reason of the shell fire they hardly knew it, the boys located the place where they had so nearly succumbed. They found the spot where their cameras had been set up, for they were marked by little piles of stones to steady the tripods. But there were no boxes of films.

"Gone!" exclaimed Blake disconsolately, as he looked about. "And we'll perhaps never get another chance to make such pictures again!"

"It surely is tough luck!" exclaimed Joe.

They saw a sentry on guard, for this place was far enough from the lines of both forces to obviate the use of trenches.

"What are you looking for, Buddies?" asked the soldier, who knew the moving picture boys.

"Some valuable army films," explained Blake, giving the details. "They're very rare, and we'll probably never get any others like them."

"Did you leave them here?"

"Right around here," answered Joe. "I think just near this pile of rocks," and he indicated the spot he meant.

"Say, now," exclaimed the American private, "I wouldn't be surprised but what those two fellows took 'em!"

"What two fellows?" cried Blake.

"Why, just as I was coming on duty here I saw two fellows, one dressed as a German soldier and the other in a blue uniform, walking around here. I thought they were up to no good, so I took a couple of shots at 'em. I don't believe I hit either of 'em, but I came so near that I made 'em jump. And then, just before they ran away, across No Man's Land, I saw them stoop down and pick up something that looked like boxes. I thought they might be something they had lost in the fight the other day, for the scrap went back and forth over this section. But now, come to think of it, they might have been boxes of your films."

"I believe they were!" cried Blake.

"What two fellows were they you saw?" asked Joe.

The soldier explained, giving as many details as he could remember, and Charlie cried:

"Lieutenant Secor for one - the chap in the blue. A French traitor!"

"He did have a uniform something like the French," admitted the private. "The other was a Fritz, though."

"Labenstein!" murmured Joe. "I wonder if it is possible that they are with the Hun army and have learned through spies that we are on this front. If they have, they would know at once that those were boxes of films, and that's why they stole them! Do you think it possible, Blake?"

CHAPTER XXI

ACROSS NO MAN'S LAND

Blake Stewart did not answer at once. He appeared to be considering what the soldier had told him. And then Blake looked across No Man's Land - that debatable ground between the two hostile forces - as though to pierce what lay beyond, back of the trenches which were held by the Germans, though, at this point, the enemy was not in sight.

"Could it, by any chance, have been Secor and Labenstein who got our films?" asked Joe.

"Very possible," agreed Blake. "Labenstein, of course, would be with the German forces, and since Secor is a traitor he would be there also. Of course it may not have been those fellows, but some other two men who had learned through their spies that we were here taking pictures and wanted them for their own purposes."

"The question is, can we get them back?" put in Charlie, scowling in the direction of the Germans.

"That's only one of the questions," observed Blake. "The main one is, where are the films now, and where did those fellows go with them?"

"Maybe I can help you out there," put in the soldier. "I saw those two fellows heading that way, down in that depression, and they certainly carried some sort of flat, square boxes under their arms."

"What's down in there?" asked Joe eagerly.

"Well, it *was* a machine-gun station, and old Fritz certainly played hob on our boys with it," answered the sentry. "But we wiped that out the other day, though I guess the dugout is there yet, or whatever is left of what they used to house their barker in. The two fellows I saw were heading for that spot."

"Is that between the lines?" asked Joe.

"Just about, yes, though there aren't any of our trenches, or theirs either, near there now. What trenches there were have been knocked into smithereens. That's No Man's Land down there. It belongs to whoever can keep it, but just now nobody seems to want it. I'm here to report if there's any movement on the part of Fritz to take up his station there again."

"As it is now, could we go down there?" asked Joe eagerly.

"Well, if you wanted to take a chance, I s'pose you could," answered the sentry slowly. "I wouldn't stop you. You don't belong to the army, anyhow, and we've been instructed that you're sort of privileged characters. All the same, it might be a bit dangerous. But don't let me stop you."

"Come on!" exclaimed Joe, starting down the slope that led across the bullet-scarred and shell-pitted ground.

"Where are you going?" asked Charles Anderson.

"Across No Man's Land," answered Joe grimly. "I'm going to see if we can get back those stolen army films. If they were ours, I wouldn't be so anxious about them. But they belong to Uncle Sam. He hired us to take them, and it was our fault they were lost."

"Not exactly our fault," put in Blake. "We couldn't help being gassed."

"No, but excuses in war don't go. We've got to get back those films!"

"That's right!" exclaimed Charlie. "I'm with you!"

"Oh, for the matter of fact, so am I," said Blake quickly. "I feel, as you do, Joe, that it's up to us to do all we can to get back those films. I'm only trying to think out the best plan for getting them."

"Go right down there and make that traitor Secor, and that submarine Dutchman, give 'em back!" cried Charlie.

"Yes, and perhaps make such a row that there'll be a general engagement," said Blake. "No; we've got to go at this a little differently from that. I'm in favor of getting the films away from those fellows, if they have them, but I think we'd better try to sneak up there first and see what the situation is. If we march down there in the open we'll probably be fired on - or gassed, and that's worse."

"Now you've said it, Buddy!" exclaimed the sentry. "I've had both happen to me, and getting shot, say in a soft place, ain't half as bad as the gas. Whew! I don't want any more! So, if I was you, I'd wait until after dark to make a trip across No Man's Land. You'll stand a better chance then of coming back alive."

"That's what I think," returned Blake, and though Joe and Charlie were eager for action, they admitted that their chum's plan was best.

"We'll have to make some preparations," Blake went on; "though I don't know that we need say anything to Captain Black about what we are going to do."

"He might stop us," said Charlie.

"Oh, no, he wouldn't do that," Joe assured their assistant.

"I'll tell you what to do," counseled the sentry: "I'm going to be on duty here until late this afternoon. I'll keep my eyes peeled for anything that may happen down there where that dugout used to be, and I'll let you know.

"Meanwhile, you can be getting ready to take a little excursion there after dark. You'd better take your gas masks with you, and also your automatics, for you may run into a party of Fritzes out to get the night air."

"That's what we'll do," decided Blake, and his chums agreed with him. And then they began to make their preparations for the perilous trip across No Man's Land that night.

They were not asked to make any pictures that day, for which they were thankful, as they still felt some of the effects of the gas, though they were rapidly improving.

Following the fight in which the boys so nearly lost their lives and in which there were severe losses on both sides, though with a net gain of territory in favor of the Allies, there was a period of comparative calm in the American ranks. The soldiers took advantage of this to rest and repair their damaged uniforms, arms and equipment. And it was on one of these days, when discipline was somewhat relaxed, that the moving picture boys made their preparations.

As they were left pretty much to themselves when they were not called on to be making pictures, it was rather easy for them, without exciting any comment, to get ready. This consisted in seeing that their automatic pistols were in good working order. They also applied for new gas masks, with a fresh impregnation of chemicals. When they received these, and with a supply of lampblack, they were ready, waiting only for the fall of darkness.

The lampblack was to be put on their hands and faces so that their whiteness would not be revealed in case the Germans played their searchlights on the ground the boys hoped to cover, or sent up star clusters to give light for raiding parties sent out to kill the French and American wounded, such being one of the pleasant ways in which Fritz makes war.

Late in the afternoon they paid a visit to their friend the sentry, asking if he had seen anything of the two men that they suspected might have the films - Secor and Labenstein.

"I wouldn't know 'em by those names even if I saw

'em," said the soldier, "and, as a matter of fact, I didn't see the same two chaps I saw before. But I have seen figures moving about down in that hollow, where we wiped out the machine gun squad, and I wouldn't be surprised but what there was something doing there."

"I only hope our films are there," said Joe.

"Don't build too much on it, Buddy," advised the sentry. "As I say, I saw some figures I took to be Germans down in that valley, but they may be getting ready for a raid on our lines, and may have nothing to do with your pictures."

"Well, we'll take a chance," decided Blake.

"That's what!" chimed in Joe.

Being accredited representatives of a certain branch of the army, though non-combatants, the boys were allowed to pass through the sentry lines, except in certain restricted places. They were given the countersign each night in case they desired to leave their quarters and go about.

But there was a risk in starting on this journey. As non-combatants, if they carried arms and went into the enemy's territory, they were not entitled to be considered prisoners of war. Of course they could fight for their lives, but not with the same status as could a uniformed soldier. As a matter of fact, they did not wear the regulation uniform, having dark suits better suited to this night excursion than the khaki.

Waiting until it was dark enough for their purpose and taking with them electric flashlights to use in case they got into a hut or some such place where they could not see to search for their films, and having blackened their hands and faces and seen that their weapons were in order, they sallied forth from the home of the humble French couple, many good wishes going with them.

It was a walk of three or four miles from the little village to the place where the sentry had said the dugout lay, and during the first part of the trip the boys talked to each other.

"Do you suppose we'll really find the films there?" ventured Joe.

"It's a slim chance, but one worth taking," said Blake. "Though I can't imagine what Secor and Labenstein, if those two fellows are really here, could want of them."

"Maybe they just picked them up on the chance that they would give away some of the American army secrets," suggested Charlie. "And they would show our boys were drilling, fighting, and all that. Of course some of the things on the films were actually seen by the Germans, but others were not; and I fancy those would be of value to Fritz. That's why they took 'em."

"They couldn't have known we were here taking views," remarked Joe.

"Oh, yes they could!" declared Blake. "Germany's spy system is the best in the world, and lots that goes on in America is known in Germany before half of our own people hear about it. But we'll have to get there before we can find out what is in that dugout, if it's there yet."

"Well, some part of it - maybe a hut or a brush heap - must be there, or the sentry wouldn't have seen men about it," observed Joe. "And now we'd better keep quiet. We're getting too close to talk much."

A little later they passed a sentry - not their friend - gave the proper password, and then stood on the edge of No Man's Land.

What would be their fate as they crossed it and ventured on the other side - the side held by the Germans?

"Come on!" whispered Blake softly, and, crouching down to avoid as much as possible being detected in the starlight, the boys went cautiously into the debatable territory.

CHAPTER XXII

CAPTURED

Not without a rather creepy feeling did the three boys start on their mission, the outcome of which could only be guessed. They were taking great risks, and they knew it. But it was not the first time. They had gone into the jungle to get films of wild beasts at the water hole. They had ventured into Earthquake Land where the forces of nature, if not of mankind, were arrayed against them. And they had dared the perils of the deep in getting pictures under the sea.

But these were as nothing compared to the mission on which they were now engaged, for, at any moment, there might go up from the German lines, not half a mile away, a string of lights that would reveal their presence to the ever-watchful snipers and sharp-shooters.

And, more than that, the whole area might suddenly be swept by a hail of bullets from a battery of machine guns. Both sides had these deadly weapons in readiness, and it was well known that Fritz was exceedingly nervous and apt, at times, to let burst a salvo of fire without any real reason.

The fluttering of some armless sleeve on the body of a

dead man, the rattle of a loose strand of barbed wire, the movement of a sorely wounded soldier lying out in the open, might draw the German fire. And if the moving picture boys were caught in that they would be hard put to it to escape.

"The only thing to do, when you see a flash of fire, is to drop to the ground and lie as still as you can," Blake had said to his chums before they started out. "Duck your heads down on your arms and don't move. The lampblack will kill any glare from the lights and they may not see us. So remember, don't move if you see anything like a light. It may be a glare from a discharged rifle, or it may be a rocket or star cluster. Just lie low, that's the way!"

And so, as they crawled on, in crouching attitudes, over the desolate stretch that lay between them and the place they sought, they made no noise, and kept a sharp watch.

Blake led the way, his hand ready on his pistol, and the other two boys followed his example. Their gas masks were ready at their belts, but these were mainly an added precaution, as it was not likely, unless a general attack was contemplated, that the Germans would produce the chlorine.

Blake had gone a little way down the slope, Joe and Charlie following as closely as was safe, when the leader came to a halt. Watching his dim form, his chums did the same.

"What is it?" whispered Joe, in the softest of voices.

"A figure," answered Blake likewise. "I'm not sure

whether it's a dead man or some one like us - trying to discover something. Do you see it?"

Joe looked. He saw a huddled heap which might, some day, have been a man. Now it was but a - heap. As the boys strained their eyes through the darkness they became aware that it was the body of a man - a French soldier who had fallen in the engagement of a few days before, and who had not yet been buried. There were many such - too many on both sides for the health and comfort of the living.

"Pass to one side," advised Joe. "We can't do him any good."

"Poor fellow!" murmured Charlie. "Ouch!" he suddenly exclaimed, in louder tones than any they had heretofore used.

"Quiet!" hissed Blake. "What's the matter?"

"A big rat ran right over my legs," answered Macaroni.

"Well, if he didn't bite you what are you yelling about?" demanded Joe. The trenches were full of rats - great, gray fellows - for there was much carrion food for them.

Once more, making a little detour, Blake started forward, but hardly had he again taken up his progress when there came the sound of a slight explosion over toward the German lines, and almost instantly the dreary stretch of No Man's Land was brightly illuminated.

"Down! Down!" hoarsely called Blake, and he and his

chums dropped full length on the ground, never heeding puddles of water, the rats or the dead, for they became aware that more bodies were all about them.

Up from the German lines went a series of rockets and star clusters. They made the battle ground between the two forces almost as bright as day, so that should any of the unfortunate wounded men be seen to move they might be killed.

Perhaps some keen-eyed Hun, watching for just this chance, had detected a slight movement near the dead man beside whom Blake and his chums first stopped. And, knowing from a previous observation that the body was cold and stark, the sniper must have reasoned that the living had joined it.

Or perhaps the incautious exclamation made by Charlie when he felt the big rat may have been carried to the ever-listening ears. However that was, the glaring lights were set off, and at once hundreds of rifles, aimed over the tops of the German trenches, began to send a hail of lead across No Man's Land.

Fortunately the line of fire was either to one side of where the boys had fallen, or it was too high or too low. They did not stop to consider which it was, but were thankful that they felt none of the leaden missiles, though some sang uncomfortably close.

For perhaps five minutes the glaring lights illuminated the blood-stained ground, and the firing was kept up at intervals. It was replied to from the American and French lines, but with what effect could only be guessed.

And then, once more, darkness settled down, and the boys began to breathe more easily. They had had a narrow escape, and their journey was not half over, to say nothing of the return trip - if they lived to make it.

"Come on!" Blake cautiously whispered again. "And bear off to the right. The fire wasn't so heavy from there. Maybe we can find a gap to get through."

His companions followed him as he crawled along, actually crawling this time, for it was not safe to rise high enough to walk even in a stooping position. No one could tell when the glaring lights might be sent up again.

But, for a time, Fritz seemed satisfied with the demonstration he had made. Perhaps he had killed some of the wounded, for not all of them had been brought in. Perhaps he had only further mutilated bodies that had long since ceased to be capable of movement.

And so, over the dark and bloody ground, Blake and his chums made their way. In a little while they would be in comparative safety, for their friend the sentry had told them there were no regular trenches near the little hollow where once had stood a machine-gun emplacement and where the boys now hoped to find their precious war films.

But their journey was not destined to be peaceful. Once more the flaring lights went up, and again came the heavy firing. Again the boys crouched to get below the storm of bullets, and again they escaped. But a groan and a cry of anguish, from somewhere on their left, told them some poor unfortunate had been put out of his misery.

They waited a little while, and then again took up the perilous journey. Presently Blake, taking a cautious observation, announced that they were in comparative safety, and might walk upright.

"Where's the hut - or whatever it is?" asked Joe.

"Down in that little hollow, I take it," said Blake. "We can't see it until we round that little hill. Maybe we can't see it at all, for it may not be there," he added. "But we'd better go slow, for it may be there, and there may be some one in it."

"Secor and Labenstein, perhaps," murmured Charlie.

"Perhaps," agreed Blake. "If they are -"

He did not finish, but his chums knew he meant there might be a desperate fight.

A little later, having proceeded cautiously, the boys made the turn around the little hill that had hitherto hidden from view the hollow of which the American sentry had spoken, and then they saw in the light of the stars what seemed to be a tumbled-down hut. As a matter of fact, it had once been a concrete dugout, where a machine gun had been placed in order to fire at the French and American lines. But in the heavy fighting of the past few days this place had been captured by an American contingent. They had destroyed the gun and killed most of the crew, and the place had been blown up by a bomb. But the fierce waves of Germans had surged back over the place, driving out the Americans who, in turn, captured it again.

Just now the place was supposed to be deserted, being of no strategic value, and in a location that made it dangerous for either side to hold it.

"We'll take a look in there," said Blake, when they had drawn near and had discovered that the ruins of the concrete dugout had been covered with brush, to "camouflage" it from spying airmen.

They approached cautiously, and, as they did so, they became aware of a faint light coming from the ruins. So faint was it that at first it seemed no more than the reflection of the stars, but a long look showed that it was a light from within, but carefully screened.

"We've got to have a look in!" whispered Blake. "Maybe the films are there, and maybe not; but some person is."

"Probably Germans," said Joe.

"Very likely. But it may be that Frenchman. If we could only capture him!"

"I'd like a chance at him!" exclaimed Charlie.

"Hush!" cautioned Blake. The boys were now close to the hut, for that was all it was since the bombardment. They tried on three sides of the place to look in, but without success. Then, as they moved around to the side which faced the German lines, they saw a crack through which the light streamed in greater volume.

"Take a look, Blake," advised Joe.

His chum did so, and, with an exclamation of surprise

and satisfaction, turned away from the slot, motioning to the others to look for themselves. And as Joe and Charlie looked they saw, seated on the ruins of a machine gun and other things that had been in the place, Secor and Labenstein. The two plotters had between them boxes which the boys had no difficulty in recognizing as their missing war films.

Joe was about to utter an exclamation of delight when Blake softly put his hand over his chum's mouth.

"Not a sound!" breathed Blake.

For a moment the boys stood looking in at the plotters and wondering how they could capture them, or at least get back the stolen films.

And then a door, or what had been a door, to the dugout swung open with a creak of its rusty hinges.

"What's that?" cried Secor, in French, starting to his feet.

"Only the wind," replied the German, in the tongue of his
fellow-conspirator. "Only the wind."

"Ah! I thought maybe it was -"

"You thought perhaps it was the boys who own these films, but who will never see them again. I know not how valuable they may be - these films - but I was told to get them, and I have. Let the ones higher up decide on their value. But we must get our price for them - you and I. We must get a good price. We have run a great risk."

"Yes, a great risk," murmured the Frenchman.

Blake motioned to his chums to follow him into the dugout. They could see his gestures in the light of a lantern which formed the illumination of the ruins.

Cautiously the three went inside, the noise they made being covered by the rattling of the wind which had sprung up.

"We have them! We have them!" exulted Joe, in a whisper.

They were silently considering how best to surprise and capture the two men, who were still unaware of the presence of the boys, when a sudden noise came from outside. Blake and his chums, as well as the two men, started.

"That was not the wind!" exclaimed Secor.

"No, my friend. It was not. I think there is some one here besides ourselves. We must look. I -"

And then came a guttural command in German:

"Surrender - all of you! You are surrounded and are prisoners! Surrender!"

CHAPTER XXIII

THE AIRSHIP RAID

Surprise on the part of Blake and his chums, as well as on the part of Secor and Labenstein, was so complete that it would be hard to say who felt the sensation most. The moving picture boys, after danger and difficulties, had found the stolen army films and those they believed had taken them. They were about to make a dash and get not only the precious boxes, but also, if possible, capture the two plotters, when, like a bolt from a clear sky, they were themselves called upon to surrender.

"Come on!" yelled Charlie, as he understood the import of the summons to surrender. "We can make a fight for it!"

"Don't try it!" advised Blake. By the light of lanterns carried by the raiding party of Germans he had seen that they were numerous and well armed. It would have been the height of folly to resist, especially as the boys were non-combatants and not entitled to the honors of war.

"Hands up - and search them!" commanded the German officer of the raiding party, as he pointed to Blake and his two chums. He spoke in German and then lapsed into English, which he spoke very well, saying:

"It will be best for you Americans to give in quietly. Hands up!" And the order was stern.

The boys had no choice but to obey, and their weapons were quickly taken from them.

"I will allow you to keep your gas masks for the present," the German captain said, "as you may need them, as we ourselves may, before we get back to our lines."

"Then we are going back with you?" asked Joe.

"Of a certainty - yes! Did you think I would leave you here to go back to your own? Indeed not! Now, then, ready - march - all of you!" and he nodded at Secor and Labenstein.

Blake and his two friends noticed that no hostility seemed directed toward the two conspirators, who, however, appeared as much surprised at the advent of the raiding party as were the boys. It was evident, though, that some understanding existed between the German captain and Labenstein, for they talked in low voices while Secor stood a little apart. The gaze of the Frenchman rested on the boys in what Blake said later seemed a peculiar manner.

"Well, up to your old spying tricks, I see!" exclaimed Joe, with a sneer he could not forego. "Have you summoned any submarines lately?"

A strange look passed over the face of the Frenchman,

but he did not reply. Labenstein, who had finished his talk with the German captain of the raiding squad, turned to the boys, and a tantalizing smile spread over his face as he said:

"Ah, we meet again, I see!"

"And you don't seem to have found much use for my flashlight," said Blake. "I hope it still works!"

The German muttered an exclamation of anger, and turned aside to pick up the boxes of films. This was too much for Charles Anderson, who sprang forward, crying:

"Say, those are ours, you Dutch thief! Let 'em alone! We came here to get 'em! Let 'em alone!"

The German captain gave a sharp order, and Charlie was forcibly pulled back by one of the soldiers.

"Say, but look here!" exclaimed the lanky assistant of the moving picture boys. "This isn't war. I mean we aren't fighting you Germans - though we might if we had the chance. We're just taking pictures, and these fellows have stolen our films," and he indicated Secor and Labenstein. The latter made some reply in German to the captain which the boys could not understand.

"Give us back our films and let us go!" demanded Macaroni. "We only came to get them!"

"Enough of this!" broke in the captain. "You are our prisoners, and you may be thankful you are alive," and he tapped his big automatic pistol significantly. "March!" he ordered.

Labenstein and Secor picked up the boxes of exposed film containing the army views and went out of the hut followed by some of the soldiers. Then the moving picture boys were told to follow, a guard of Germans, with ready bayonets, closing up the rear. A little later the boys, prisoners in the midst of the raiding party, were out under the silent stars. For the time peace had settled over the battlefield, extending across the trenches on both sides.

"I wonder what they are going to do with us," said Joe, in a low voice, to Blake.

"Hard to tell," was the quiet answer. "They're marching us toward their lines, though."

This was indeed true, the advance being toward a section of the field beyond the German trenches whence, not long before, had come the searchlights and the hail of shrapnel.

"Well, things didn't exactly turn out the way we expected," said Charlie. "I guess we'll have to make a re-take in getting back our films," he added, with grim humor. "How do you figure it out, Blake?"

The talk of the boys was not rebuked by their German captors, and indeed the captain seemed to be deep in some conversation with Secor and Labenstein.

"I don't know how it happened," Blake answered, "unless they saw us go into that hut and crept up on us."

"They crept up, all right," muttered Joe. "I never heard a sound until they called on us to surrender," he added.

"Maybe Secor and Labenstein saw us and never let on, and then sent a signal telling the others to come and get us," suggested Charlie.

"I hardly think that," replied Blake. "The Frenchman and his fellow German plotter seemed to be as much surprised as we were. You could see that."

"I guess you're right," admitted Joe. "But what does it all mean, anyhow?"

"Well, as nearly as I can figure it out," responded Blake, as he and his chums marched onward in the darkness, "Secor and Labenstein must have hidden the films in the hut after they stole them from the place where we went down under the gas attack. For some reason they did not at once turn them over to the German command."

"Maybe they wanted to hold them out and get the best offer they could for our property," suggested Charlie.

"Maybe," assented Blake. "Whatever their game was," and he spoke in a low tone which could not carry to the two plotters who were walking ahead with the German captain, "they went to the hut to get the films they had left there. And as luck would have it, we came on the scene at the same time."

"I wish we'd been a little ahead of time," complained Macaroni. "Then we might have gotten back with our films."

"No use crying over a broken milk bottle," remarked Joe.

"That's right," Blake said. "Anyhow, there we were and there Secor and his German friend were when the others came and -"

"Here we are now!" finished Joe grimly.

And there, indeed, they were, prisoners, with what fate in store none of them could say.

Suddenly from the darkness a sentinel challenged in German, and the captain of the little party answered, passing on with the prisoners.

A little later they turned down into a sort of trench and went along this, the boys being so placed that each walked between two Germans, who carried their guns with bayonets fixed, as though they would use them on the slightest provocation. But Blake and his chums gave none.

And then, making a sudden turn, the party came to what was evidently an outpost of importance. There were several large underground chambers, fitted up with some degree of comfort and a number of officers and soldiers about. Some were eating, some smoking, and others drinking, and still others sleeping. In one room could be seen a rough table, laden with maps and papers, and there were many electric lights, showing to what degree of perfection the German military system was carried out at this point. A portable dynamo and gasolene engine probably furnished the current.

The captives were halted, and a brief talk in German took place between the captain and the officer to whom he reported. What was said Blake and his chums could not, of course, hear, nor could they have understood had they heard.

A little later, however, they were ordered to march on, and then were shown into an underground room, none too clean and quite dark, and the door was banged shut on them. Just before this they had seen Secor and Labenstein go off in another direction, still carrying the boxes of films.

The echoes of the retreating footsteps of the men who had thrust them into their prison soon died away, and the boys were left to themselves in a veritable cell that was unpleasantly dirty and dark.

"Whew!" whistled Joe, after a moment of silence. "This time we certainly are up against it!"

Suddenly a light flashed in the darkness.

"What's that?" asked Joe sharply.

"I want to see what sort of hotel accommodations they've given us," was Blake's grim answer, as he flashed his pocket light about. The Germans had not taken those from the boys, and they were soon inspecting their prison.

It was merely a hole dug underground, earth, supported by timbers, forming the floor, ceiling and sides, while the entrance was made of a plank door, with cracks large enough to show that a passage ran outside - a passage along which men passed with a frequency which seemed to indicate that escape would be exceedingly difficult.

"Well, we've just got to make the best of it," said

Blake. "I'm going to get what rest I can."

It could not be much at best, for there was no furniture in the cavelike cell. The boys curled up in corners - fortunately it was not cold - and thought over their situation. That it was very desperate they all admitted.

That night was like a bad dream to them. At times they dozed off in light slumber, but, as far as they knew, their captors did not so much as look in on them. They did not know, of course, when morning came, but they judged that the sun had risen when, after several hours of waiting, a tin can of water and some food was thrust in to them.

"And I'm hungry enough to eat even German sausage," announced Macaroni, as he inspected the food. It was coarse but satisfying, and the boys felt better when they had eaten it.

Later came a squad of Germans, one of whom spoke enough English to order Blake and his chums to follow them. They were led out of the dungeon, along a covered underground passage, and then they suddenly emerged into daylight.

"Well, it's a comfort to be able to see," remarked Joe, as he and his companions looked about.

Without a word as to where they were to be taken, the boys were marched along, and, for a moment, they feared they were to be the victims of a firing party. But a turn in the course showed them just ahead a group of buildings about which could be seen some German officers.

"Evidently we're going to be questioned by some one in authority," suggested Blake. "Well, that looks more hopeful."

They were at the very edge of an enclosure containing the official headquarters of that part of the German army, and the leader of their squad was about to reply to the challenge of the sentinel when a curious sound was borne to the ears of the boys. It was like a fast motor operating at some distance.

"What's that?" asked Charlie.

As if by a common impulse they all looked up, for the noise seemed to come from above, and they saw dotting the blue sky many small, black specks.

"Aeroplanes!" cried Blake.

The Germans had seen the objects in the air at the same time, but on them the sight produced quite a different effect from that made on the boys.

In an instant all thought of guarding Blake and his chums seemed to have been forgotten. Their escort ran to one side. The sentries on duty before the official headquarters hastened away, and some of the elaborately gold-laced officers ran within the buildings.

A moment later a number of soldiers could be observed some distance away manning a battery of guns, the muzzles of which pointed upward.

"They're going to fire at the airships!" cried Joe.

"And that means they are not German craft!" added

Blake. "Boys, I guess the French and Americans are making an airship raid on Mr. Fritz this morning, and maybe it'll be a good thing for us. Let's hunt cover!"

CHAPTER XXIV

BURIED ALIVE

Even as Blake and his chums looked about for some place of refuge, the firing of the German anti-aircraft guns began. These weapons, designed especially for shooting straight up and sending shrapnel shells to a considerable height, were rapidly manned and fired by crews that seemed to be in readiness for just such danger.

The raid of the French and American airships, quickly as the defensive preparations were made, seemed to take the Germans by surprise. That is the only way the boys could account for the fact that their guarding escort deserted them. For deserted they had been, some of the Germans running back in the direction whence Blake and the others had come, while a few, under orders from one of the German officers, helped to man the guns of which several score were now shooting at the aircraft high above the Hun position.

Joe, Blake and Charlie paused a moment, before seeking some shelter, to watch the thrilling sight. On came the aeroplanes, like a flock of great birds, and they did not resemble anything else quite so much, high up as they were. They came on in regular formation, for the day of the lone attack by an aeroplane was passed, except under special circumstances.

Straight for the German camp - if camp it could be called - came the flying squadron. As yet the airships were too high to be hit by the German guns, however great their range.

But the airships came on. Their speed was not apparent at so great a height, but it must have been wonderful, for but a few minutes seemed to have elapsed from the time they were first sighted, far down on the horizon, until they were almost overhead.

"And now's the time for us to get under cover!" said Blake. "When they begin to drop bombs, there'll be something doing around here."

"Where'll we go?" asked Charlie.

"Oh, there ought to be plenty of bomb-proofs and dug-outs in this camp. The Germans must have been air-raided before, or they wouldn't have the anti guns ready. The most likely place to find the best cyclone cellars will be near the officers' headquarters, I think. Trust those fellows to have a safe place ready."

"Do you think they are making the raid to help us?" asked Joe.

"Hardly," replied Blake. "They probably don't even know that we have been captured. No, I guess this has been in preparation on our side for some time, judging by the number of craft in it. I hope they wipe out this dump!"

"But not until we get under cover!" said Joe. "Look!

There goes one of our ships!"

As he spoke a white cloud seemed to burst in the vicinity of one of the aircraft. The machine, which with the others had come lower down, was seen to dip and plunge. Then, after what seemed a dizzy fall, it straightened out again and kept up with the others.

"Hit but not disabled," murmured Blake, as he and his chums paused in their race for shelter. "The Germans are getting the range, I guess."

"Why don't we drop some bombs?" cried Joe, speaking as though he and his friends were personally engaged.

"I guess they're waiting until they get in a favorable position," returned Blake. "Look out! Here comes one!"

Something black dropped from one of the airships. It fell in a long curve, landing in a spot which the boys could not see, and an instant later there was a terrific explosion.

"That hit an ammunition dump, all right!" cried Charlie. "Duck, fellows!"

"In here!" yelled Blake, for at that moment they came opposite what looked like the entrance to a tunnel. It was lighted by small electric lamps and appeared to extend some distance into the earth. No one could be seen in it or entering it as the boys made a dive for it.

And it was well that Blake, Joe and their assistant found shelter when they did, for an instant later the whole area was under bombardment by the airships.

The boys, racing through the tunnel, dug underground and timbered and braced as is a mine shaft, could not see what went on, but they could hear and imagine.

By this time the American and French aeroplanes were directly over the German camp and were dropping tons of explosives. The bombs struck and burst, some of them setting off stores of ammunition and powerful powder designed for the big guns. And these explosions, combined with the firing of the weapons aimed to bring down the flying enemy, made a pandemonium which penetrated even to the tunnel along which the boys were fleeing.

"That's some fight out there!" cried Joe.

"If we could only film it!" added Charlie, his voice and that of his chum ringing hollow in the tunnel.

"We'd stand about as much chance as we did when the volcano let loose in Earthquake Land," answered Blake. "Come on, fellows! This isn't over yet."

"I only hope we don't run into a party of Huns who'll drive us out," murmured Joe.

But, so far, they had met no one, though ahead of them they could hear a sound as though others were running through the underground shaft seeking a place of safety.

"Where are we going, anyhow?" asked Charlie at length.

"Going until we stop," answered Joe.

"And that'll be soon," added Blake, "for I see the last of the lights."

The boys looked down the long passage, which was well made and was high enough to permit them to run upright. It was wide enough, also, for three to go abreast. As Blake had said, the string of incandescent lights, suspended overhead, came to an end a little farther on. They stopped under the third light from the last and looked about them.

"Isn't this as good a place as any?" asked Joe. "If we go on any farther we may get into a hole we can't get out of. I say, let's stay here. We'll be safe from the airship bombs."

"I don't know about that," said Blake. "If you'll notice, we have come along pretty much on the level. This tunnel wasn't dug in the side of a hill. It went into the ground slanting, and at such a gradual slope that the top can't be very far under the surface."

"What does that mean?" asked Charlie.

"It means that we haven't much dirt over our heads, and if a bomb were to drop directly above us we'd be in a bad way. I think we'd better keep on until we get to a deeper part of the cave, or whatever it is."

"But we'll have to go on in the dark," objected Joe. "There are only three more lights, and -"

Suddenly came a muffled explosion, and the lights went out, leaving the place in black gloom.

"Now there aren't any lights," said Charlie, when the

echo of the dull roar had passed away. The tunnel had been shaken, and there was a pattering sound all about the boys, as if little particles of earth had been dislodged, but no other damage appeared to have been done.

"It *is* dark!" said Blake. "But come on. Use your pocket lights. No, hold on. We'll use only one at a time. No telling how long we may need them."

Bringing out his own light, he flashed it on and led the way. Above them a continuous roar could now be heard, and they guessed that the airships were attacking in force, directly over the German camp, and were being fired at from all sides.

"One bomb must have splattered Fritz's electric plant," observed Joe, as he and his chums hurried on as best they could in the somewhat dim light of the little pocket lamp Blake carried.

Hardly had he spoken when there came a tremendous explosion - one that staggered the boys and seemed to crumple up the tunnel as though it were made of paper.

They had no time to cry out. They were thrown down and felt rocks and stones falling about them, while their ears were deafened by the roaring sound.

Then came silence and darkness - a darkness that weighed heavily on them all, while Blake, who had been in the lead, tried to move his hand to flash on the electric light that had gone out or been broken. He could barely move, and as he felt dirt and rocks all about him there was borne to his senses the horrible message:

"Buried alive!"

After that thought mercifully came unconsciousness.

CHAPTER XXV

THE END OF LABENSTEIN

How long they lay entombed in the German tunnel the moving picture boys did not know. They must have been unconscious for some time.

Joe was the first to regain his senses. Telling about it later, he said he dreamed that he had been taking views in Earthquake Land and that, somehow or other, a volcano had fallen on his chest. He had difficulty in breathing, and no wonder, for as he came to his senses he found that a great rock and a pile of earth were across him.

Slowly at first, fearing to move much because he might bring down more debris on himself, Joe felt about. He found that his arms and hands were comparatively free, though partly buried in earth.

"I say!" he called, and his voice sounded strange in that dark and broken tunnel, "is any one here but me? Blake! Charlie! Are you alive?"

No one answered, and then, feeling his strength coming back, Joe ventured to move. He found that he could manage to emerge from the pile of earth and stones that had fallen on him, fortunately none over his head. When he ventured to stand upright he tried to pierce the darkness and find out what had become of his chums.

But he could see nothing until he thought of his pocket lamp and, taking it in his hand, flashed it about him. The light revealed to him the figures of Blake and Charlie, lying not far away and covered with debris as he had been.

He set the little light on a rock, leaving the switch on, and by the intense but limited glow, he set to work to free his companions. Blake's head was bleeding from the cut of a sharp rock, but he, like Joe and Charlie, had fallen in such a way, or rather, the cave-in had taken place in such a manner, that their heads and faces were comparatively free from dirt, else they would have been smothered.

Joe worked feverishly to free his chums and at length succeeded in freeing his assistant, who, of the two, was less covered by the debris. Charlie opened his eyes and looked about him, asking:

"What happened? Where am I?"

"Don't stop to ask questions now," directed Joe. "Help me with Blake. I'm afraid he's hurt!"

The two together got their chum cleared of the debris finally, and then Joe, taking a flask of cold coffee from his pocket, gave his now half-unconscious chum some to drink. This served further to rouse Blake, and it was soon found, aside from a painful cut on the head, that he was uninjured except for bruises, such as they all had.

"But what happened?" asked Charlie, as they sat down to rest on some rocks and took turns finishing Joe's limited supply of coffee.

"The tunnel caved in on us after a big explosion of some kind," Joe said. "I guess we're going to have trouble getting out, too."

"Let's have a look," suggested Blake. "We can't stay in here much longer or more of the roof and sides may cave in. Can we get out?"

"I haven't looked," answered Joe. "I wanted to get the dirt off you fellows. I'm afraid we're caught, though."

And they were. An examination, made with the pocket lights, showed them that the way back was blocked by a mass of rock and earth and that no progress ahead could be made for the same reason.

"I guess we'll have to dig our way out," said Joe.

"What with?" asked Charlie.

"Some of the broken boards that held up the tunnel," was the answer, and Joe pointed to pieces of timber that had been splintered and shattered by the cave-in.

"Yes, it's the only way out," agreed Blake, who, now that his cut had been bound up with bandages from the first-aid kits the boys carried, felt better. "We'll have to dig out." And after a short rest they began this work.

A terrible fear was upon them, a fear greater than that caused by their capture by the Germans with the possibility of being shot as spies. It was the fear of a horrible death - buried alive.

They dug as best they could for some time with the broken boards, their hands becoming cut and bruised by the rough edges. And yet, with all their efforts, they could not see that they had gained much.

They were digging back along the way they had come in, for, as Blake said, they knew how long the tunnel was in that direction, but they did not know how far it extended the other way.

"Is it of any use to continue?" asked Joe wearily, when they had been digging for what seemed several hours, though really it was not as long as that.

"Of course we've got to continue!" declared Blake, half savagely. "We can't give up now - and die!"

"We may die anyhow," said Joe.

They were resting in the darkness after strenuous digging. In the dark because, to save the battery, they had switched off the electric light by which they had been working.

Charlie turned to look back. They had been piling the earth behind them as they worked, but there was not much of it as yet. They had made but small impression on the debris that hemmed them in. And as Charlie looked he uttered a cry.

"What is it?" asked Blake.

"A light! Don't you see a light there?" Charlie demanded. "See! Back there through the chinks in the rock. See, a flickering light!"

There was no doubt of it! There was a gleam of light, and it appeared to come from a point where some fallen rocks were loosely piled.

Dropping their boards, which they had been using for shovels, the boys climbed as near as they could to the hole. In the dark as they were, the light showed plainly. "Can you see anything?" asked Charlie of Joe, who was nearest.

"No, only some figures moving about. It seems like some sort of dugout beyond there, and it hasn't caved in. Maybe it's the end of the tunnel."

"Did you say you can see somebody in there?" asked Blake.

"Yes; figures moving about."

"Call to them."

"Maybe they're Germans!" exclaimed Charlie.

"They probably are," Blake answered. "But we've got to be rescued from here and take our chance with them. It's better than being buried alive. Hello, there!" he shouted. "Help us get out!" and he began tearing at the stones with his hands.

Seeing his object, his chums helped him. And then some one on the other side of the rocky barrier also began pulling down the stones, so that in a little while, the light becoming momentarily greater, the boys saw a way of escape open to them.

But it was a strange way. For when the rocks had been pulled down sufficiently to enable them to crawl through, they emerged into a space - a small room, as it were - walled with solid logs. Logs also formed the roof. It was a room lighted by a lantern, and on a pile of bags in one corner lay a huddled figure of a man. Standing near him was another man - a man in a ragged blue uniform - and at the sight of his face Blake murmured:

"Lieutenant Secor!"

"At your service!" said the Frenchman, bowing slightly.

"No!" bitterly cried Blake. "Not at *our* service - you traitor!"

The Frenchman seemed to wince, but at that moment a call from the huddled man in the corner attracted his attention. He bent over him, drew back the covering and revealed in the lantern's glow the face of Labenstein.

The German raised himself on one elbow, and a wild look came over his face. His eyes gleamed brightly for a moment.

"They - they here!" he murmured. "Well, perhaps it is better so."

"How better? What does he mean?" asked Blake. "Does he think -"

"Hush!" and the Frenchman spoke softly. "This is the end - of Labenstein!" And even as he spoke the man fell back dead.

Lieutenant Secor seemed to breathe a sigh of relief, as though the death of the other had brought a great release to him.

"Now I can speak," said the officer. "Now I can explain, and perhaps you will again regard me as a friend," he said softly.

"Well," returned Blake, "you probably saved our lives by helping us get out of the tunnel. But as for being friends with -"

"Please do not say it," begged the lieutenant. "I have had to play a part. It is over now. I can again take my place with my comrades and fight openly for France. For I have learned all his secrets and whence the spy-leaks came. Now my unpleasant mission is over!"

"What - what do you mean?" asked Joe, beginning, as did his chums, to have an inkling of the truth. "Aren't you two working together against us and for Germany?"

"Never I!" cried the Frenchman. "I am a member of the French Secret Service, and for months I have consorted with that dog!" and he pointed at the dead man. "I but played a part to gain his confidence and to learn from what sources Germany was getting her secret information about our soldiers and yours. Now I know. I will explain. But come, we must get out of here."

"Can we get out?" asked Blake.

"Surely, yes. The tunnel goes from here into the

German trenches, and the other end was not damaged by the explosion."

"But," exclaimed Joe, "the German trenches! We don't want to go there to be captured again."

"Have no fear," said the Frenchman, with a smile. "I should, perhaps, have said what *were* the German trenches. They are now held by some of your own troops - the brave Americans!"

"They are?" cried Charlie.

"That is true! You shall see!"

"Hurrah!" cried the moving picture boys, and their fears and weariness seemed to depart from them in a moment.

"The great airship raid was a sucess," went on the Frenchman. "Our troops and yours have made a big advance, and have captured many prisoners. They would have had Labenstein, but he is beyond prisons now. Let us go hence! Even dead I can not endure his company. I suffered much on his account."

"Well, things are happening so fast I don't know which to begin to think of first," remarked Joe. "But, on general principles, I presume it's a good thing to get out of this tunnel. Come on, boys."

"One moment," interposed the lieutenant. "Perhaps you will like to take these with you."

He stooped and lifted a pile of trench bags, and the boys saw the boxes of moving picture films.

"Ours?" cried Joe.

"None else," answered the Frenchman. "I trust you will find them all right."

"Not a seal broken!" reported Charlie, who had quickly examined the cases. "This is great!"

Together, hardly able to believe their good luck, they made their way out of the log-protected room - once a German bomb-proof dugout. As they emerged into the trenches, carrying the films, the boys saw American soldiers.

"The Stars and Stripes!" cried Charlie, as he noted the United States flag. "Now we're all right!"

"Whew! We did make some advance!" added Blake, as they saw how the battle lines of the French and Americans had been extended since they had crawled into No Man's Land the night before.

The boys learned later that the airship raid was the forerunner of a big offensive that had been carried out when they were held prisoners and in the tunnel. The Germans had been driven back with heavy loss, and one of their ammunition dumps, or storage places, had been blown up, which had caused the collapse of the tunnel.

That the moving picture boys were welcomed by the soldiers, among whom they had many friends, goes without saying. And the recovery of the films was a matter for congratulation, for they were considered very valuable to the army.

"Though it was Lieutenant Secor who really saved them for us," explained Blake, when the story of their adventure was being told.

"And I am glad the time has come when Lieutenant Secor can appear in his true light," said Captain Black. "Even I suspected him, and he lost many friends who will come back to him, now that he risked all to serve his country in a role seldom honored - that of getting secret intelligence from the enemy."

For that is what the French lieutenant had been doing. Even while he was in the United States, where the boys first met him, he had been playing that part.

"But I assure you," he said to Blake and the others, "that the destruction of your films by my auto was an accident. When I found you believed it done purposely I let it go that way, as it helped me play my part the better. Also, I had to act in a manner to make you believe I was a friend of Labenstein. But that was all a part."

And it had not been an easy part for the French officer to play. He had, in ways of his own, come to suspect Labenstein, who went under various names, sometimes that of Karl Kooder. This man, who held forged citizenship papers of the United States, was a German spy and had done much to aid the Kaiser. But he accepted Lieutenant Secor as a co-worker, on the latter's representation that he, too, was a friend of Germany, or rather, as the Frenchman made Labenstein think, was willing to become so for a sum of money. So the two seemingly worked together.

"And it was thus you knew us," said the lieutenant to

the boys. "Labenstein, to use one of his names, had orders to make all the trouble he could for you when you reached France, and to prevent your getting any pictures, if possible. Of course he could not do that, but he tried, even to the extent of writing a false note in London that caused your arrest. I had, seemingly, to help him, but all the while I was endeavoring to find out where the leak was on our side that enabled him to profit. And I found out. The leak will be stopped.

"I even seemed to join Labenstein in signaling the submarine, though that night, had he really succeeded in calling her with your light, I would have killed him where he stood. However, the depth charge solved that question.

"I had to escape from the ship with him to lull his suspicions against me. Then I went into the German ranks with him, being thought a deserter! That was hard for me, but I had my duty to perform.

"The rest you know. It was by a mere chance that Labenstein, when I was with him, came upon your films after the gas attack. He thought to profit personally from selling them, which is why he did not turn them over at once to his superiors. Ever since then he has been trying to dispose of them to enrich himself. And I have been trying to find a way to get them back to you without betraying myself and my mission.

"At last chance favored me. The big air attack came just after I had secured all the information I wanted. I was about to go back to my comrades and arrange for the capture of Labenstein if I could. He still had the films and was about to sell them to another German - a traitor like himself.

"Then came the big explosion, and he was fatally hurt. We both took refuge in the tunnel, Labenstein carrying with him the films, and you came just as Labenstein died. Well, perhaps it is better so."

"Yes," agreed Blake, "I think it is."

"And we have the films back!" exulted Charlie.

"But, best of all, we know Lieutenant Secor is straight!" cried Joe. "I'd hate to think anything else of him, after he saved our lives."

"Yes," agreed Blake softly.

"And now to get back on the job!" cried Joe, after a moment of silence.

And so the moving picture boys again took up their perilous calling. They soon recovered from their slight injuries caused by the cave-in of the tunnel, and, finding their cameras where they had left them in the French house, resumed the turning of the cranks.

They filmed many stirring scenes, and the records they made now form an important part of the archives of the War Office in Washington, the films so strangely lost and recovered being considered most valuable.

Lieutenant Secor became one of the boys' firmest friends, and through his help they were enabled to obtain many rare views. And now, having seen them safely through some of their perils, we will take leave of them.

George Eliot
George Gissing
George MacDonald
George Meredith
George Orwell
George Sylvester Viereck
George Tucker
George W. Cable
George Wharton James
Gertrude Atherton
Gordon Casserly
Grace E. King
Grace Gallatin
Grace Greenwood
Grant Allen
Guillermo A. Sherwell
Gulielma Zollinger
Gustav Flaubert
H. A. Cody
H. B. Irving
H.C. Bailey
H. G. Wells
H. H. Munro
H. Irving Hancock
H. Rider Haggard
H. W. C. Davis
Haldeman Julius
Hall Caine
Hamilton Wright Mabie
Hans Christian Andersen
Harold Avery
Harold McGrath
Harriet Beecher Stowe
Harry Castlemon
Harry Coghill
Harry Houidini
Hayden Carruth
Helent Hunt Jackson
Helen Nicolay
Hendrik Conscience
Hendy David Thoreau
Henri Barbusse
Henrik Ibsen
Henry Adams
Henry Ford
Henry Frost
Henry James
Henry Jones Ford
Henry Seton Merriman
Henry W Longfellow
Herbert A. Giles

Herbert Carter
Herbert N. Casson
Herman Hesse
Hildegard G. Frey
Homer
Honore De Balzac
Horace B. Day
Horace Walpole
Horatio Alger Jr.
Howard Pyle
Howard R. Garis
Hugh Lofting
Hugh Walpole
Humphry Ward
Ian Maclaren
Inez Haynes Gillmore
Irving Bacheller
Isabel Hornibrook
Israel Abrahams
Ivan Turgenev
J.G.Austin
J. Henri Fabre
J. M. Barrie
J. Macdonald Oxley
J. S. Fletcher
J. S. Knowles
J. Storer Clouston
Jack London
Jacob Abbott
James Allen
James Andrews
James Baldwin
James Branch Cabell
James DeMille
James Joyce
James Lane Allen
James Lane Allen
James Oliver Curwood
James Oppenheim
James Otis
James R. Driscoll
Jane Austen
Jane L. Stewart
Janet Aldridge
Jens Peter Jacobsen
Jerome K. Jerome
John Burroughs
John Cournos
John F. Kennedy
John Gay
John Glasworthy

John Habberton
John Joy Bell
John Kendrick Bangs
John Milton
John Philip Sousa
Jonas Lauritz Idemil Lie
Jonathan Swift
Joseph A. Altsheler
Joseph Carey
Joseph Conrad
Joseph E. Badger Jr
Joseph Hergesheimer
Joseph Jacobs
Jules Vernes
Julian Hawthrone
Julie A Lippmann
Justin Huntly McCarthy
Kakuzo Okakura
Kenneth Grahame
Kenneth McGaffey
Kate Langley Bosher
Kate Langley Bosher
Katherine Cecil Thurston
Katherine Stokes
L. A. Abbot
L. T. Meade
L. Frank Baum
Latta Griswold
Laura Dent Crane
Laura Lee Hope
Laurence Housman
Lawrence Beasley
Leo Tolstoy
Leonid Andreyev
Lewis Carroll
Lewis Sperry Chafer
Lilian Bell
Lloyd Osbourne
Louis Hughes
Louis Tracy
Louisa May Alcott
Lucy Fitch Perkins
Lucy Maud Montgomery
Luther Benson
Lydia Miller Middleton
Lyndon Orr
M. Corvus
M. H. Adams
Margaret E. Sangster
Margret Howth
Margaret Vandercook

Margret Penrose
Maria Edgeworth
Maria Thompson Daviess
Mariano Azuela
Marion Polk Angellotti
Mark Overton
Mark Twain
Mary Austin
Mary Catherine Crowley
Mary Cole
Mary Hastings Bradley
Mary Roberts Rinehart
Mary Rowlandson
M. Wollstonecraft Shelley
Maud Lindsay
Max Beerbohm
Myra Kelly
Nathaniel Hawthrone
Nicolo Machiavelli
O. F. Walton
Oscar Wilde
Owen Johnson
P.G. Wodehouse
Paul and Mabel Thorne
Paul G. Tomlinson
Paul Severing
Percy Brebner
Peter B. Kyne
Plato
R. Derby Holmes
R. L. Stevenson
R. S. Ball
Rabindranath Tagore
Rahul Alvares
Ralph Bonehill
Ralph Henry Barbour
Ralph Victor
Ralph Waldo Emmerson
Rene Descartes
Rex Beach
Rex E. Beach
Richard Harding Davis
Richard Jefferies
Richard Le Gallienne
Robert Barr
Robert Frost
Robert Gordon Anderson
Robert L. Drake
Robert Lansing
Robert Lynd
Robert Michael Ballantyne
Robert W. Chambers
Rosa Nouchette Carey
Rudyard Kipling
Samuel B. Allison
Samuel Hopkins Adams
Sarah Bernhardt
Sarah C. Hallowell
Selma Lagerlof
Sherwood Anderson
Sigmund Freud
Standish O'Grady
Stanley Weyman
Stella Benson
Stella M. Francis
Stephen Crane
Stewart Edward White
Stijn Streuvels
Swami Abhedananda
Swami Parmananda
T. S. Ackland
T. S. Arthur
The Princess Der Ling
Thomas A. Janvier
Thomas A Kempis
Thomas Anderton
Thomas Bailey Aldrich
Thomas Bulfinch
Thomas De Quincey
Thomas Dixon
Thomas H. Huxley
Thomas Hardy
Thomas More
Thornton W. Burgess
U. S. Grant
Valentine Williams
Various Authors
Vaughan Kester
Victor Appleton
Victoria Cross
Virginia Woolf
Wadsworth Camp
Walter Camp
Walter Scott
Washington Irving
Wilbur Lawton
Wilkie Collins
Willa Cather
Willard F. Baker
William Dean Howells
William le Queux
W. Makepeace Thackeray
William W. Walter
William Shakespeare
Winston Churchill
Yei Theodora Ozaki
Yogi Ramacharaka
Young E. Allison
Zane Grey

www.ingramcontent.com/pod-product-compliance
Lightning Source LLC
LaVergne TN
LVHW090604110826
845146LV00001B/255

* 9 7 8 1 4 2 1 8 2 4 5 9 8 *